AF575282

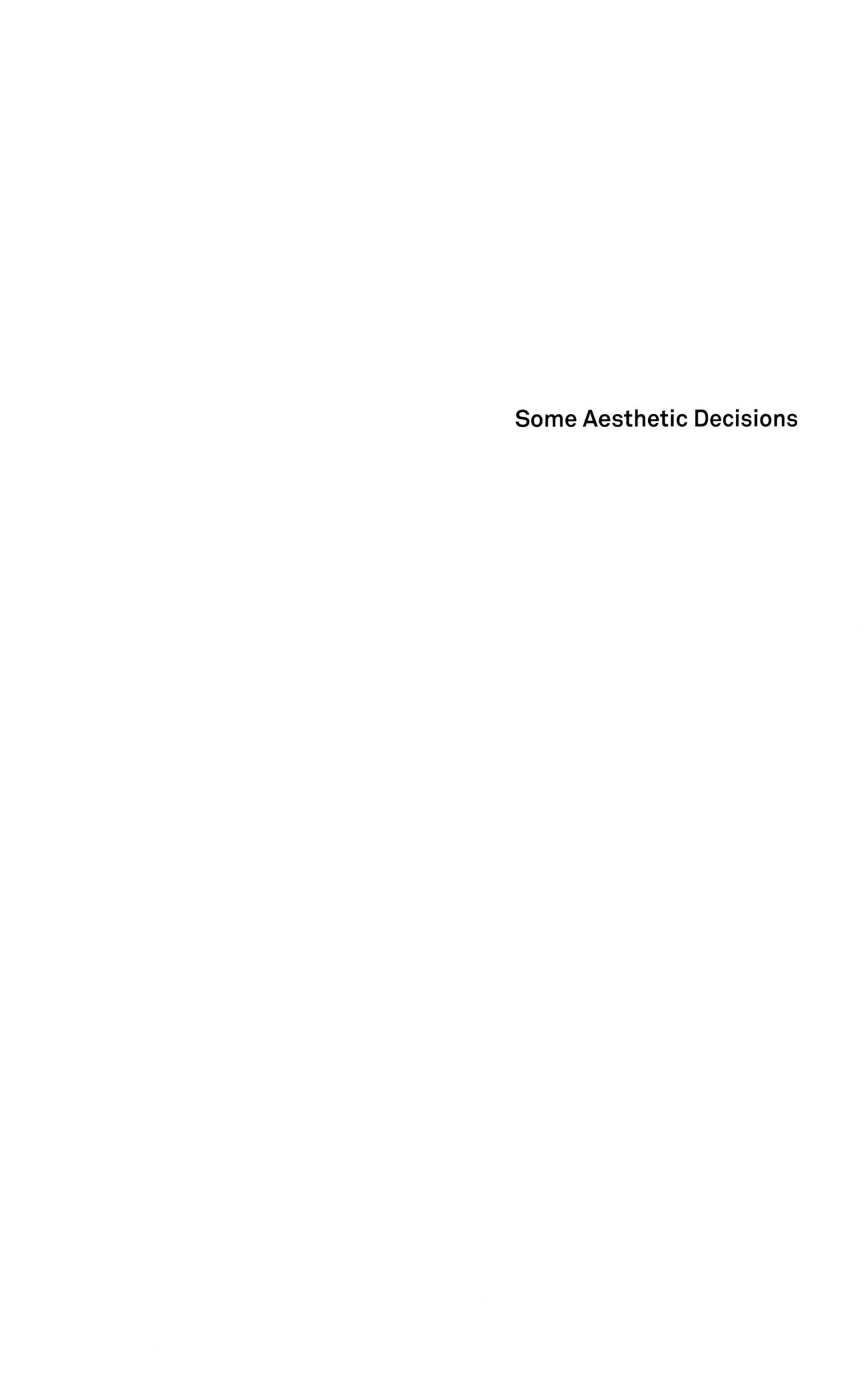

# Some Aesthetic Decisions

# Some Aesthetic Decisions

*A Centennial Celebration of Marcel Duchamp's "Fountain"*

Bonnie Clearwater

*with additional essays by*

Francis M. Naumann and Laurette E. McCarthy

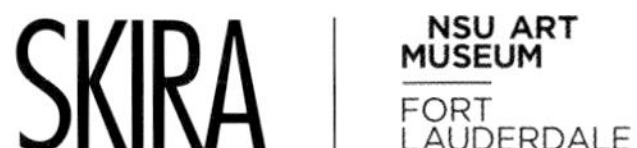

*Cover*
Rachel Lachowicz
*Untitled (Lipstick Urinals)*, 1992
Detail of pl. 7

*Art Director*
Marcello Francone

*Design*
Luigi Fiore

*Editorial Coordination*
Emma Cavazzini

*Copy Editor*
Doriana Comerlati

First published in Italy in 2017 by
Skira editore S.p.A.
Palazzo Casati Stampa
via Torino 61
20123 Milano
Italy
www.skira.net



Printed and bound in Italy. First edition

ISBN: 978-88-572-3623-0 (NSU Art Museum Fort Lauderdale)
ISBN: 978-88-572-3479-3 (Skira editore)

Distributed in USA, Canada, Central & South America by Rizzoli International Publications, Inc., 300 Park Avenue South, New York, NY 10010, USA.
Distributed elsewhere in the world by Thames and Hudson Ltd., 181A High Holborn, London WC1V 7QX, United Kingdom.

This exhibition is organized by
NSU Art Museum Fort Lauderdale
One East Las Olas Boulevard,
Fort Lauderdale, Florida 33301

May 14 – September 3, 2017

*Curator*
Bonnie Clearwater
Director and Chief Curator,
NSU Art Museum
Fort Lauderdale

Exhibitions and programs at NSU Art Museum Fort Lauderdale are made possible in part by a challenge grant from the David and Francie Horvitz Family Foundation and John S. and James L. Knight Foundation. Funding is also provided by Nova Southeastern University, Broward County Board of County Commissioners as recommended by the Broward Cultural Council and Greater Fort Lauderdale Convention & Visitors Bureau, the State of Florida, Department of State, Division of Cultural Affairs and the Florida Council on Arts and Culture. NSU Art Museum is accredited by the American Alliance of Museums.

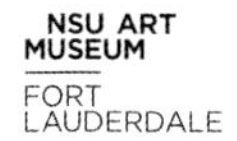

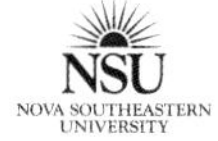


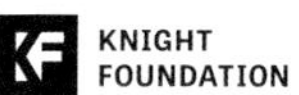

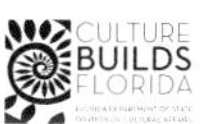

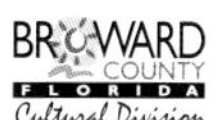

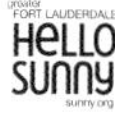

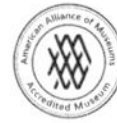

## List of Lenders

Steven Baldi
The Broad, Los Angeles, CA
Castelli Gallery, New York, NY
Dillon L. Cohen
de la Cruz Collection, Miami, FL
Judy Fiskin
Richard and Elyse Froehlich Collection
Gagosian Gallery, New York, NY
Jeff and Mei Sze Greene Collection
David Horvitz and Francie Bishop Good
The Institute of Contemporary Art/Boston, Boston, MA
Rosalind and Melvin Jacobs Collection
Koenig & Clinton, New York, NY
Joseph Kosuth
Alex Melamid
Metropolitan Museum of Art, New York, NY
Francis M. Naumann Fine Art, LLC, New York, NY
Pérez Art Museum Miami, Miami, FL
The Collection of John & Amy Phelan
The John and Mable Ringling Museum of Art, Sarasota, FL
Rubell Family Collection, Miami, FL
Julian Schnabel
Shoshana Wayne Gallery, Los Angeles, CA
Dr. and Mrs. Barry Silverman
Thomas Solomon and Kimberly Mascola
Stuart and Judy Spence
Sprüth Magers, London
Team (Gallery, Inc.), New York, NY
Richard Telles Fine Art, Los Angeles, CA
Walker Art Center, Minneapolis, MN
The Andy Warhol Museum, Pittsburgh, PA

Dada artist Marcel Duchamp forever changed the nature of art when he submitted *Fountain*, a porcelain urinal signed "R. Mutt," for the Society of Independent Artists exhibition in New York (April 10 to May 6, 1917). This exhibition was an open call to artists in which any submission would be shown. Duchamp, who was on the SIA board, tested the limits of the organization's guidelines by anonymously presenting what would become his most famous readymade (an ordinary manufactured object that he designated as a work of art). The subsequent rejection of Duchamp's *Fountain* by the exhibition's organizers ignited a controversy that continues today about the definition of art and who gets to pass judgment.

The exhibition *Some Aesthetic Decisions: A Centennial Celebration of Marcel Duchamp's "Fountain"* appropriates the title of a series of photographs by Los Angeles artist Judy Fiskin, and is fittingly a "readymade" title in the spirit of Duchamp's revolutionary action for creating art—choosing an existing object and elevating it from its everyday use to the realm of art. With this gesture he created a new thought about the found object and redirected the consideration of the art work from a visual experience to an equally pleasurable cerebral experience. His maneuver was simple, yet so complex that it is one of the most significant influences on the field of contemporary art. Therefore the emphasis on *Some* in the title of the exhibition applies to the need to focus on a selection of artists. The rest of the title, *Aesthetic Decisions*, also refines the selection to artists for whom the active act of choosing and making deliberate decisions led to a new thinking about the aesthetic condition.

On a personal note, I have been planning an exhibition exploring the topic of aesthetics since I first saw Sophie Calle's series, *The Blind*, in an exhibition at Fred Hoffman Gallery, Santa Monica, 1989, the same year I was researching and editing the book *West Coast Duchamp* (Miami Beach: Grassfield Press, 1991). I had scheduled presenting an exhibition under the title *Some Aesthetic Decisions* several times over the years, but decided it was not the right moment. In the interim I kept adding (and eliminating) artists to my list for the show, including Fiskin, and added her title to my title in the 1990s. When I realized that 2017 was the centenary of *Fountain*, I knew it was the right time to present this exhibition. The archaic spelling of "aesthetic" in this publication reflects my own aesthetic decision; I prefer how "aesthetic" looks visually rather than "esthetic."

I would like to extend my deep appreciation to the artists included in this exhibition as their work continues to generate new thoughts for me. I am indebted to the many private collectors and my colleagues at the various museums and art galleries who so generously loaned works. I also thank the esteemed Duchamp scholar Francis M. Naumann and noted authority on the Society of Independent Artists Laurette E. McCarthy for contributing essays on these subjects for this publication. I extend my appreciation to the staff at NSU Art Museum Fort Lauderdale, including Senior Curator Dr. Barbara Buhler Lynes, Exhibitions and Curatorial Project Manager Diana Blanco, Assistant Registrar Aleesha Ast, and Christopher Albert, Head Preparator. Many thanks to James A. Clearwater and Sue Henger for their editorial guidance. At Skira, Milan, I would like to thank Emma Cavazzini, Doriana Comerlati, and Giuseppina Leone, for their dedication to this beautiful publication.

As always, the museum's Board of Governors, chaired by David W. Horvitz, has been exceptionally supportive and encouraging. At Nova Southeastern University, I extend my gratitude to Dr. George L. Hanbury, II, President and CEO, and Dr. Jacqueline A. Travisano, Executive Vice-President and Chief Operating Officer, for all their assistance.

Bonnie Clearwater
*Director and Chief Curator*
*NSU Art Museum Fort Lauderdale*

# Contents

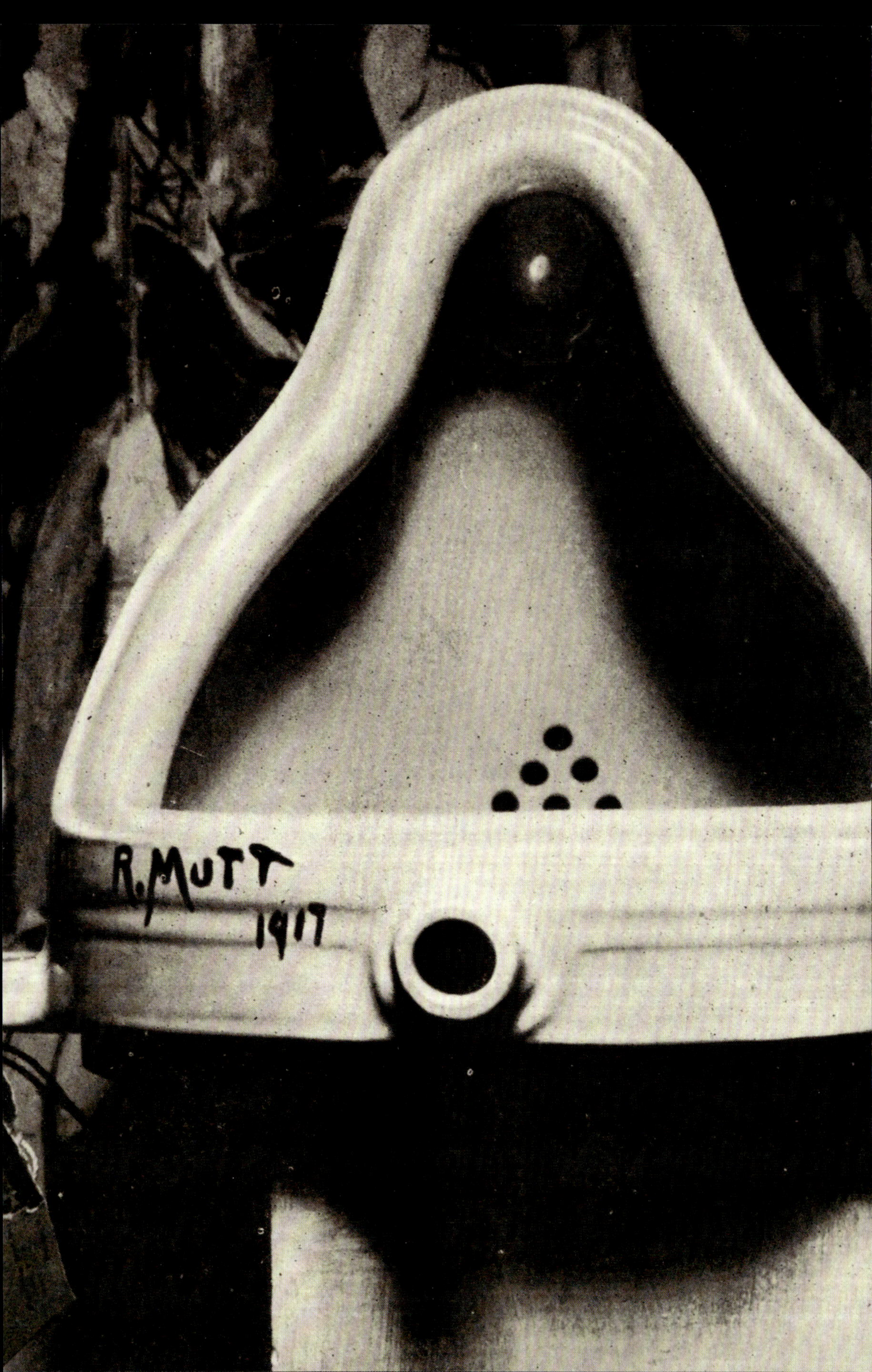
R. MUTT
1917

*Bonnie Clearwater*

# The Mysterious Case of Richard Mutt

One hundred years ago, Marcel Duchamp anonymously submitted his notorious work *Fountain*, a mass-produced urinal, to the American Society of Independent Artists (SIA) in New York (pl. 1). Modeled after the Société des Artistes Indépendants in Paris, the SIA declared that any artist who paid the initiation fee of one dollar and annual dues of five dollars could enter works for display in this juryless exhibition that aimed to show the widest array of styles and schools.[1] No work would be rejected. No awards would be bestowed.

Duchamp, who was a founder of the SIA and was on its board and exhibitions hanging committee, tested the limits of the organization's guidelines by submitting *Fountain* to the show. The subsequent rejection of this work by the board on grounds of indecency ignited a controversy that persists to this day about the definition of art and who gets to pass judgment.

*Fountain* and other manufactured and found objects that Duchamp commandeered as art works with little or no alteration formed a new classification of art he called "readymades." While this act alone had a dramatic impact on the course of contemporary art, this exhibition, *Some Aesthetic Decisions: A Centennial Celebration of Marcel Duchamp's "Fountain,"* specifically addresses the nature of *Fountain*'s origin as rooted in the artist's conscious act of choosing.

After *Fountain* was rejected, Duchamp and a number of other members of the board resigned. This scandalous defection was splashed in the papers, which piqued the public's interest in the exhibition. Duchamp arranged to have Alfred Stieglitz, a champion of photography and modern art in America, photograph *Fountain*, and it was delivered to his studio some time before April 19, 1917. As the original *Fountain* disappeared soon after it was photographed, Stieglitz's picture contributed significantly to shaping the debate over the meaning of the work and the artist's intentions. In this photograph, the urinal is precariously perched on a small pedestal in front of a painting by Marsden Hartley (*The Warriors*, 1913).[2] Stieglitz's dramatic lighting emphasizes the urinal's sensuous curves, and casts a shadow at the top left. To some, the urinal in the photograph looked like a veiled Madonna or a statue of a Buddha, an association reinforced by Louise Norton in her article published with Stieglitz's photograph in the art journal *The*

Alfred Stieglitz
*Fountain*, 1917
Detail of pl. 1

*Blind Man*.[3] As William Camfield points out in his extensive study of *Fountain*, the reproduction of this work in *The Blind Man* gave the public its first glimpse of a work that thus far was known only through rumor.[4]

Stieglitz's stylized photograph of *Fountain* was widely reproduced (mostly after 1959), and consequently it perpetuated the argument that the artist intended to draw attention to the formal beauty that could be discovered in the most mundane objects. Duchamp's intention, however, ran counter to this defense. As he later admitted, he deliberately selected the object because it lacked any inherent beauty, stating that "the choice of these 'Readymades' was never dictated by esthetic delectation. This choice was based on a reaction of visual indifference with at the same time a total absence of good or bad taste . . . in fact a complete anesthesia."[5] Duchamp made the distinction that taste is acquired; it becomes a force of habit in which art is measured against the highest recognized standards within a period of a culture. Duchamp aimed to break himself of the habit of taste by deliberately selecting objects that held no particular visual interest. He did not always succeed in his goal to avoid tasteful judgments as some of the readymades, especially the *Bottle Rack*, 1914, are among the most formally appealing modern sculptures (or perhaps Duchamp shaped our taste for utilitarian objects).

A second defense of *Fountain* published along with the Stieglitz photograph in *The Blind Man* offered an alternative interpretation of the controversial work. "The Richard Mutt Case," a short statement submitted without a by-line, proposed that it was the artist's act of choosing that was significant to the meaning of this work. The author noted: "Whether Mr. Mutt with his own hands made the fountain or not has no importance. He CHOSE IT. He took an ordinary article of life, placed it so that its useful significance disappeared under the new title and point of view—created a new thought for that object."[6] Although Duchamp never took credit for this statement, he later admitted he agreed with its sentiment.[7]

The author of "The Richard Mutt Case" limited the act of choosing to the artist's selection of the object. However, the creation of *Fountain* was the product of numerous choices, including the decisions to enter the urinal in an art exhibition, to give the work a title, to invent a name for the artist, and to sign and date the work (the signature also suggests reorienting it 90 degrees to a non-utilitarian position, as photographed by Stieglitz). By choosing to enter *Fountain* into an art exhibition, Duchamp made his intentions clear that this particular urinal was now classified as a work of art. The signature and date declare that this plumbing fixture is unique, as it has been claimed by an artist as a work of art. Giving the object a title elevated its status as well. In this case, the choice of the title itself redirected the spectator's focus to conceptualizing the work through the intellect or imagination rather than through sight alone. Years later (in

1966), he explained that the short sentences he added to a number of the readymades (for example, he added the phrase "In advance of the broken arm" to a snow shovel) were "meant to carry the mind of the spectator towards other regions more verbal" than visual.[8] The title *Fountain* prompts the viewer to envision a functioning fountain, but it also implants in the mind the actual use of this apparatus as a receptacle for a stream of urine.[9]

It is this last impression that most disturbed the board of the SIA as they rejected it on the grounds of indecency. It was "obscene" in the classical Greek-drama definition of the word: a violent or crude action occurring "off scene" or "off stage" yet taking form in the spectator's imagination. Defenders of *Fountain* disputed the claim that it was "vulgar" and asserted it was no more immoral than a bathtub; but Duchamp did not choose to submit a bathtub. Rather he chose a urinal knowing it would fire up the viewer's imagination like no other object. Earlier readymades, which had been previously exhibited and known among his circle prior to the exhibition in 1917, including several members of the board of the SIA, had already made the case that an existing object could be transformed into a work of art simply by the artist's choice and decree. These early readymades were generally neutral in nature—a bicycle wheel on a stool, a snow shovel, a bottle dryer, a comb, etc. *Fountain*, however, likely contributed to a theory Duchamp advanced in 1949 concerning the artistic act as a "trinity: artist, work of art, recognition."[10] With *Fountain*, Duchamp reshuffled the viewer's role from that of a passive observer of a work of art to that of an active participant in its function. As he noted in 1957, "All in all, the creative act is not performed by the artist alone; the spectator brings the work in contact with the external world by deciphering and interpreting its inner qualifications and thus adds his contribution to the creative act."[11] Those who imagined *Fountain* to be immoral or obscene, or those who recognized it as a "new thought," had actively contributed to the creative act, and therefore were essential to its completion as a work of art.

Submitting *Fountain* under the alias "R. Mutt," concealing his authorship from the SIA board and even his friends, may have fulfilled another condition of Duchamp's philosophy of aesthetics as it pertained to the role of the spectator. At "The Western Round Table on Modern Art" symposium held in San Francisco in 1949, Duchamp proposed that only a few spectators have the ability to be receptive to the sensation that a work of art emits, which he called its "aesthetic echo." He further remarked that "the 'victim' of an aesthetic echo is in a position comparable to that of a man in love or a believer who dismisses automatically his demanding ego and, helpless, submits to a pleasurable and mysterious construct." He observed that taste and the capacity for experiencing the aesthetic echo were two different things: "Taste gives a sensuous feeling, not an aesthetic emotion." The person of taste, according to Duchamp, judges a work of art according to established opinions and standards, but individuals who experience the aesthetic shock cannot control themselves. They "submit" and "become humble" before the art work.[12] *Fountain* certainly gave viewers a jolt and, as the author of "Buddha of the Bathroom," Louise Norton, noted, "*Fountain* was not made by a plumber but by the force of an imagination; and of imagination it has been said, 'All men are shocked by it and some overthrown by it.'"[13] Because the initial audience for *Fountain*, the SIA board, presumably did not know that their friend and colleague created and submitted the work, Duchamp was able to objectively study their response to this enigmatic work. Those who assessed it according to the conventions of "taste" included: members who proclaimed *Fountain* immoral; Stieglitz, who applied his modernist sensibility to aestheticize the object in his photograph; and the author of "Buddha of the Bathroom," who extolled its formal qualities. The anonymous author (or authors) of "The Richard Mutt Case" may have been among the few who were receptive to *Fountain*'s aesthetic echo.[14]

One of the SIA co-founders and board members, artist Katherine S. Dreier, explained to Duchamp in a letter dated April 13, 1917, why she voted to reject *Fountain*: "When I voted 'No,' I voted on the question of originality—I did not see anything pertaining to originality in it—that does not mean that if my attention had been drawn to what was original by those who could see it, that I could not also have seen it."[15] Dreier's confession may have contributed to an observation Duchamp presented later, at "The Western Round Table on Modern Art," in 1949, that although enlightened art criticism and interpretive text might aid the public's understanding of modern art, no amount of exposure and education could condition a viewer who is unequipped to receive an aesthetic shock.[16] He used the analogy of an individual with color blindness who can see neither red nor green or who is unable to savor the taste of an orange. He conceded that it may be possible to make someone aware of the aesthetic echo, much as "you can almost describe the taste of an orange, and when the man tastes an orange he will see what you meant [sic]."[17]

Duchamp guided a number of adventuresome collectors of the avant-garde, including Dreier, with whom he and Surrealist Man Ray had founded the modern art organization Société Anonyme in 1920. By the time he made his statement regarding the aesthetic echo in 1949, he had had years of experience observing the responses of art spectators. One might conclude from his 1949 statement that some of his closest friends and associates never fully experienced the aesthetic shock, even after he drew their attention to the originality of a work (to paraphrase Dreier's letter).[18]

The flurry of written accounts concerning *Fountain* around the time it was rejected by the SIA—including statements by Duchamp, by board members of the society, and by the authors who defended the work in *The Blind Man*—produced so many contradictory stories that one might conclude that they were deliberately conflicting. So much confusion, in such a brief time, by such a small group of colleagues closely associated with the artist himself is suspicious. What is one to make of the multiple accounts that call into question whether Duchamp created the work? He even wrote to his sister Suzanne in Paris that he submitted it on behalf of a woman friend using the male pseudonym, Richard Mutt, adding that after the board rejected the work "I handed in my resignation and it'll be a juicy piece of gossip in New York."[19] Duchamp gleefully anticipated the scandal the chain of events would ignite. Is it possible that this small group of friends and colleagues, wittingly or unknowingly abetted Duchamp in this ruse? We know from a letter Dreier sent to the society's president William Glackens that she and Glackens conspired to have Dreier recommend to the board that they extend invitations to both Duchamp and Mr. Mutt to discuss the merits of *Fountain* (at which time one, both, or neither of them knew that inviting Mr. Mutt was impossible).[20] The authorship of the two contradictory defenses of the work in *The Blind Man* is also a mystery, although all the usual suspects were part of Duchamp's circle. Duchamp's close friend Beatrice Wood coordinated the photo shoot at Stieglitz's studio and likely had a hand in "The Richard Mutt Case" as she constantly insisted.[21] Duchamp's major patron, collector and fellow board member of the SIA, Walter Arensberg, and artist Joseph Stella, apparently were in on it right from the beginning when the urinal was selected.[22] The story that Glackens smashed *Fountain* (the account is detailed in Francis Naumann's essay in this catalog; however no one witnessed Glackens dropping the work) is attributed to fellow society board member Charles Prendergast, while Duchamp later claimed that Arensberg bought the original and subsequently lost it.[23]

Just maybe Duchamp fanned these mysteries and conflicting stories as a way to keep *Fountain*'s significance activated long after the controversy around it died down. These ambiguities are among the reasons why, one hundred years later, art historians, critics, artists, and the public are still contemplating this work. In this regard, the mysteries were essential to Duchamp's preoccupation with his quandary as to how to extend the life of his works for a posthumous, "ideal" audience.[24] In an interview at the time of his first retrospective held at the Pasadena Art Museum in 1963, Duchamp remarked that the aesthetic "lies in the sort of flavor that a painting or art work has when it has just been completed—like the aroma of a flower that has just bloomed. This aura disappears after a number of years and the impression the work makes on the spectator becomes the invention, not of the artist, but of the spectator and what he has been taught in his youth."[25] To illustrate this phenomenon, Duchamp could well have pointed to his painting *Nude Descending a Staircase, No. 2*, 1912, which had become an icon of modern art known primarily for the scandal it caused at the Armory

Show in New York in 1913. Duchamp controlled access to *Fountain* right from the beginning. In its first days of life (April 1917), *Fountain* was seen only by members of the SIA board and some of Duchamp's and Stieglitz's friends in the photographer's studio. As previously mentioned, the press covered the controversy over its rejection from the exhibition but never mentioned that the object in question was a urinal. By the time Stieglitz's photograph was published in May 1917, the work had apparently vanished, however, two photographs of his New York apartment/studio, ca. 1917, show a urinal dangling from above along with other readymades (figs. 1, 2, pp. 22–23).

Over the years, several replicas of *Fountain* were produced. The first of these were the miniature urinals created for his retrospective in a box, *The Box in a Valise (Of or by Marcel Duchamp or Rrose Sélavy)*; these boxes were made over the period 1935 to around 1961 (pl. 2). The first full-scale replica of *Fountain* was produced by Sidney Janis in 1950. This and other replicas were manufactured urinals selected by others and approved by Duchamp (each was unique in that they were from various manufacturers, and none was identical to the piece submitted to the exhibition in 1917). All of these replicas were signed "R. Mutt" with the 1917 date, reinforcing the significance of the original idea that spawned the work.

Not long after Duchamp's retrospective exhibition in Pasadena in 1963, Galleria Schwarz in Milan published a limited edition of several of his readymades, including *Fountain* and *Trap* (pl. 3). By this time, issues raised by the readymades had become all too familiar, but the limited editions inspired new debates. By producing these multiples, the objects were no longer unique art works, as was the case of the original readymades. Whereas the first ones were the product of the artist's choice to elevate everyday objects to works of art, and the latter were individual and varied common objects already in existence and decreed by the artist as replicas, the Galleria Schwarz multiples were created using the art tradition of reproduction in a limited edition. *Fountain* was constructed according to blueprints derived from photographs of the lost original, rather than from the existing object. The edition of *Fountain* was never functional as plumbing. Francis Naumann has pointed out that while Duchamp's invention of the readymades altered the traditional definition of art, the creation of each subsequent readymade incorporated subtle changes in its concept, thereby challenging even how the term "readymade" is defined.[26]

Duchamp's replicas of *Fountain* (as well as of his other readymades) demonstrated that his original concept of choosing objects to elevate to the status of fine art opened many avenues to explore. The aesthetics of the work was not limited to the artist's choice of the urinal that he used; rather it was shaped by the multitude of decisions discussed above. To succeed as a transformative art work, it was necessary for Duchamp to shroud *Fountain* in mystery, select an object that would actively engage the viewer's imagination, test the judgment of his peers, and be rejected so it could cause a scandal that would ignite rumor and innuendo. He also needed it to disappear. Just when its aura was in risk of running out in the early 1960s (as a result of his new celebrity status), the limited editions of 1964 infused *Fountain* with new life.

[1] *The Blind Man*, no. 2 (May 1917), was published by Duchamp and his friends Henri-Pierre Roché and Beatrice Wood as a forum for opinions and comments on the SIA exhibition. Announcement entitled "The Society of Independent Artists, Inc.," undated, in the Archives of the Society Anonyme, Beinecke Rare Book and Manuscript Library, Yale University, New Haven, CT. Excerpt in William A. Camfield, *Marcel Duchamp Fountain* (Houston: Houston Fine Art Press, 1989), p. 19.

[2] Francis M. Naumann, "The Big Show: The First Exhibition of the Society of Independent Artists," parts I and II, *Artforum* 17, no. 6 (February 1979), pp. 34–39, and 17, no. 8 (April 1979), pp. 49–53; and Camfield, *Marcel Duchamp Fountain*, are thorough and extensive resources on Marcel Duchamp's *Fountain*.

[3] *The Blind Man*, no. 2 (May 1917), see note 1.

[4] Camfield, pp. 27–28, notes that the urinal was never described in the press and was referred to with the general innocuous term of "bathroom fixture."

[5] Marcel Duchamp, "Apropos of 'Readymades'," talk delivered at the Museum of Modern Art, New York, October 19, 1961, in Michel Sanouillet and Elmer Peterson, eds., *The Writings of Marcel Duchamp* (New York: Da Capo, 1989), p. 141. Reprint, originally published: *Salt Seller* (New York: Oxford University Press, 1973).

[6] Camfield, p. 38.

[7] Camfield, p. 37.

[8] Duchamp, "Apropos of 'Readymades'," p. 141.

[9] Francis M. Naumann and Hector Obalk, eds., *Affectionately, Marcel: The Selected Correspondence of Marcel Duchamp* (Ghent and Amsterdam: Ludion), 2000, p. 47. In this letter to his sister Suzanne, dated April 11, 1917, Duchamp insisted there was nothing immoral about *Fountain*. However, it is notable that he used other titles and objects throughout his career that directed the spectator's mind to bodily functions and sexual acts; for instance, *The Bride Stripped Bare by Her Bachelors, Even (The Large Glass)*, 1915–23; the 1921 assisted readymade, *Why Not Sneeze Rose Sélavy* ("sneeze" in French and English is a euphemism for "orgasm"); and *Feuille de vigne femelle (Female Fig Leaf)*, 1950, a galvanized plaster cast of female genitalia. In a 1966 interview Duchamp said the alias R. Mutt was based on the name of the company that manufactured the urinal, J. L. Mott Iron Works, but he substituted Mutt from the popular *Mutt and Jeff* comic strip. He added "Richard" as the first name as it is slang for "money-bags" in French (see Camfield, p. 23).

[10] Marcel Duchamp's edited transcript of "The Western Round Table on Modern Art," San Francisco, 1949, photocopy available at the Archives of American Art, Smithsonian Institution, Washington, DC.; excerpted in Bonnie Clearwater, ed., *West Coast Duchamp*, "Appendix A" (Miami Beach: Grassfield Press, 1991), p. 111.

[11] *West Coast Duchamp*, "Appendix A," pp. 106-107.

[12] *West Coast Duchamp*, "Appendix A," p. 107.

[13] Camfield, p. 39.

[14] Although Wood consistently claimed authorship of "The Richard Mutt Case," Camfield suggests it could have been a collaborative effort of Wood, Roché, and Duchamp (see Camfield, p. 39).

[15] Camfield, p. 31.

[16] See footnote by Naumann in *Affectionately, Marcel*, p. 46: while Dreier "failed to fully comprehend the more profound philosophical implications of Duchamp's work, that did not prevent her from admiring and collecting it."

[17] *West Coast Duchamp*, "Appendix A," p. 112.

[18] In a debate with Andrew C. Ritchie, director of painting and sculpture at the Museum of Modern Art, New York, during "The Western Round Table on Modern Art," in 1949, Duchamp agreed that as it is the rare individual who has the capacity to experience the aesthetic echo and there is no means to determine who is predisposed to this trait, museums should present art to as broad a public as possible. *West Coast Duchamp*, "Appendix A," p. 111.

[19] *Affectionately, Marcel*, p. 47.

[20] *Affectionately, Marcel*, p. 31.

[21] Wood's diary records how closely she, Roché, and Duchamp worked together on the exhibition and *The Blind Man* no. 2 (see Camfield, p. 23.)

[22] Camfield, p. 21.

[23] Camfield, p. 13.

[24] *West Coast Duchamp*, p. 7.

[25] Henry J. Seldes, "Gamesmanship of Art and Life—Marcel Duchamp Style," *Los Angeles Times*, October 13, 1963, Calendar: p. 15.

[26] Francis M. Naumann in conversation with the author in 1990.

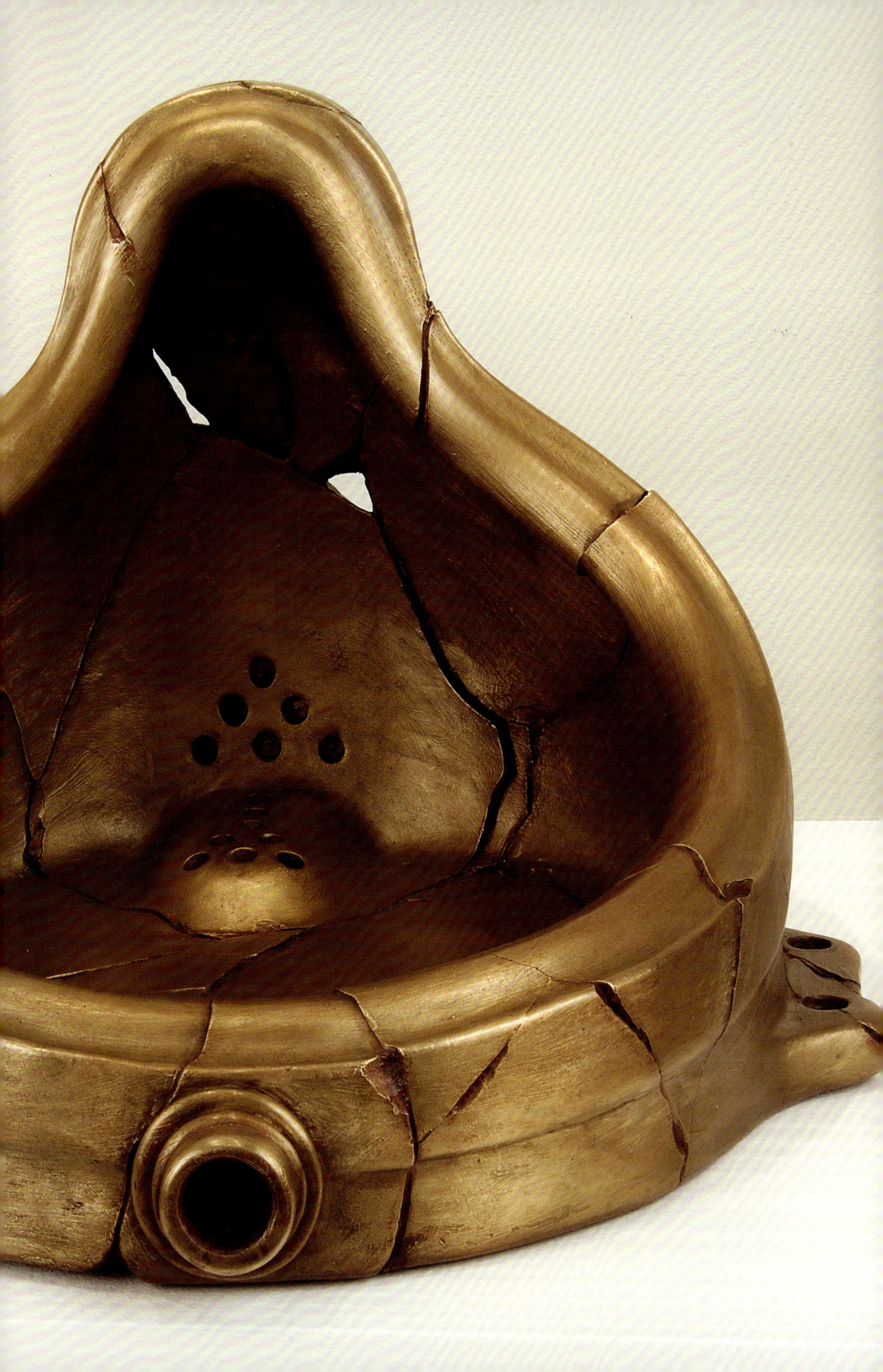

*Francis M. Naumann*

# *Fountain*'s Furtive Fate or Far-fetched Fiction?

It could be argued that the most influential work of art created by any artist in the modern era is a glistening white porcelain urinal selected by Marcel Duchamp and submitted under the name of R. Mutt to the first exhibition of the Society of Independent Artists (SIA) in New York in April 1917. On grounds of public indecency, the item was withheld from display, causing Duchamp and his patron Walter Arensberg to resign from the society, an organization they had helped to establish. Once they learned that the object would not be exhibited, Duchamp and a group of friends retrieved it from the SIA's location at the Grand Central Palace on Lexington Avenue and brought to Alfred Stieglitz, the pioneering photographer and art dealer, whose gallery was located at 291 Fifth Avenue, about fifteen blocks away. They wanted Stieglitz to take a picture of the urinal for inclusion in *The Blindman*, a magazine they published in conjunction with the SIA exhibition (spelled differently for the second and last issue: *The Blind Man*). They needed an image of the urinal to accompany an editorial they were preparing in defense of R. Mutt's submission (for, at the time, they had not yet publicly disclosed that Duchamp was its author). Stieglitz placed the object on a base that was smaller than its width (probably all he had available in the gallery) in front of a painting in his inventory by Marsden Hartley (*The Warriors*, 1913), and positioned the urinal on its back so that R. Mutt's signature and the date could be easily read. He then highlighted it from one side, causing some to think the resultant image looked like a Madonna or Buddha (pl. 1), but shortly after the picture was taken, the urinal disappeared, never to be seen again.

Exactly what happened to this controversial artifact has never been determined. Most believe that Duchamp took it home with him and hung it from the lintel of a doorway in his studio on West 67th Street (which was located on a floor directly above the Arensberg apartment), as it appears in two photographs (figs. 1, 2). Moreover, it is assumed that these photographs were taken sometime after Stieglitz took his picture but before Duchamp departed for Buenos Aires in August 1918, whereupon it is further assumed that the urinal was simply discarded. As logical as these assumptions may be, there is yet another scenario that I believe should be considered, one that posits that *Fountain* was not lost or discarded, but rather, physically

Mike Bidlo
*Fractured Fountain*
*(Not Duchamp Fountain 1917)*,
2015
Detail of pl. 6

destroyed, smashed to pieces by the president of the SIA, William Glackens.

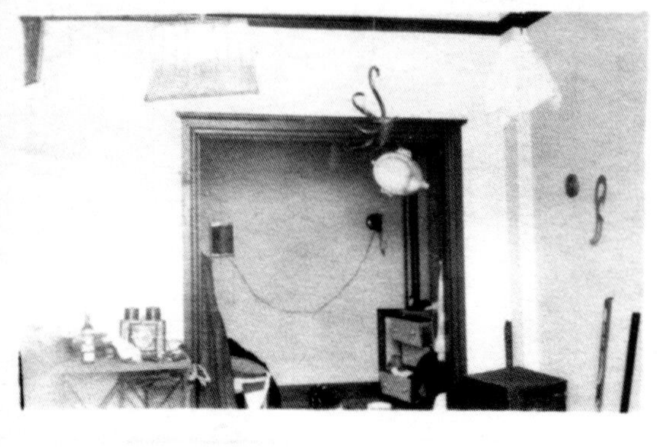

A few days before the SIA exhibition was scheduled to open, we know that R. Mutt's entry generated a great deal of controversy among the organizers. Apparently, a heated discussion erupted among the society's directors over the worthiness of a plumbing fixture being declared as a work of art, an argument witnessed by the artist Beatrice Wood, who, with Duchamp and his friend Henri-Pierre Roché, were editors of *The Blindman*. "You mean to say, if a man sent in horse manure glued to a canvas that we would have to accept it?" quipped George Bellows, the American painter who served as one of the society's directors. "I'm afraid we would," responded Walter Arensberg, who was not only a managing director of the exhibition, but one of its principal guarantors. "It is gross, offensive," argued Bellows. "There is such a thing as decency."[1] Bellows seems to have won the battle, as it was decided that the urinal could not be placed on public display, whereupon Duchamp and Arensberg tendered their resignations from the society. When the catalog appeared, R. Mutt's name was not listed among the nearly 2,000 artists included in the show. A day after the exhibition opened to the public, a notice appeared in the press with the headline "His Art Too Crude for Independents" (fig. 3), providing an explanation for why R. Mutt's urinal was excluded from the show. "The Fountain," proclaimed the organizers, "may be a very useful object in its place, but its place is not in an art exhibition, and it is, by no definition, a work of art."[2]

Fig. 1. *Duchamp studio interior*, ca. 1917
Gelatin silver print
Collection Jean-Jacques Lebel, Paris
Shown hanging above: *In Advance of a Broken Arm*, 1915; to the right of center: *Hat Rack*, 1917; hanging behind it from the lintel of the doorway: verso of *Fountain*, 1917

But was *Fountain* excluded from the exhibition? When Duchamp was asked about it years later, he explained that the work was not actually rejected, but rather suppressed from view. "The 'Fountain' was simply placed behind a partition and, for the duration of the exhibition, I didn't know where it was." He then added, "After the exhibition, we found the 'Fountain' again, behind a partition, and I retrieved it!"[3] This story was corroborated in an interview conducted with the artist Theresa Bernstein, who attended the exhibition and recalled having seen the urinal "on a staircase landing, behind a curtain."[4] In an interview with Harriet, Carroll, and Sidney Janis that took place in 1953, Duchamp was more specific about what occurred: "The thing was taken away and put somewhere, we couldn't find it for three days so we went [to the SIA exhibition] and I don't know who was there, not Stella, Stella didn't find, somebody else found it behind a partition, it had been dropped in back of a partition and forgotten, you see there were partitions in that Grand Central [Palace] building where the show was taking place and you couldn't see it. When we found it we took it out and took it back to my place."[5]

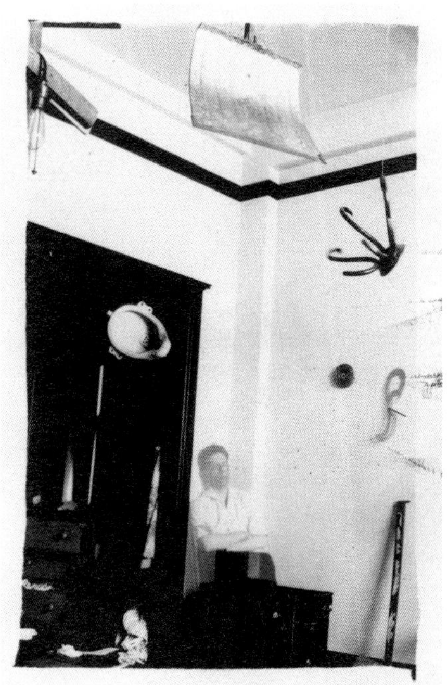

Fig. 2. *Duchamp studio interior*, ca. 1917
Gelatin silver print
Collection Jean-Jacques Lebel, Paris
Shown hanging above center: blade of the shovel titled *In Advance of a Broken Arm*, 1915; to the right: *Hat Rack*; hanging from the lintel of the doorway: recto of *Fountain*, 1917, with the ghostly image of Henri-Pierre Roché seated in corner

The only inconsistency in this account is that we know from the diary of Beatrice Wood that on April 13, 1917—three days after the exhibition opened its doors to the public—she had gone with Duchamp to "see Stieglitz about 'Fountain'." They brought the urinal itself with them, as Stieglitz took his memorable picture of it sometime within the next six days. On April 19th he wrote to the critic Henry McBride, inviting him to stop over to the gallery and see his photograph of the urinal as well as the object itself. "The Fountain is here, too," he told him, adding that he had taken the photograph "at the request of Roché, Covert, Miss Wood, Duchamp & Co."[6]

At this point, all traces of the urinal disappear, unless we accept Duchamp's recollection that it was brought back to his studio and photographs showing it hanging from the lintel of a doorway (figs. 1, 2) were taken after April 1917. In the same interview with the Janis family quoted above, Duchamp described one of these photographs as "the urinal hanging down *after* the show," so it would seem that to the best of his recollection, it was brought back to his studio after the show closed.[7] Normally, Duchamp's recollections are very precise, and there would be no reason to doubt this one were it not for the fact that we are then left in the position of having to explain what happened to the urinal subsequently. When Duchamp left his studio in 1918, he wrote to Roché asking him to retrieve some items that he had left on a balcony in the Arensberg apartment: a painting by Louis Michel Eilshemius, a package of *Blindman* magazines, and some drawings by Beatrice Wood.[8] He never mentioned the urinal, or, for that matter, any of the other readymades that are visible in the studio photographs. It is possible that he had already given them to the Arensbergs, but then what did they do with them? It would be hard to imagine that the already impassioned collector of works by Duchamp would have disposed of them, particularly the urinal, since it had caused such a furor at the SIA exhibition in which he had himself participated. There is the possibility that Duchamp discarded them, but that, too, is unlikely, considering what an important role these artifacts had played in his work (no less in the history of aesthetics, for they served to definitively alter all prior definitions of art). There is another scenario that I had originally dismissed, but which gains in credibility as it provides a succinct explanation of how the object so suddenly and mysteriously disappeared.

Charles Prendergast, who served as vice-president of the Society of Independent Artists, liked to tell the story that another controversial item was submitted to the show that he described as "a chamber pot, tastefully decorated." According to Ira Glackens, the son of William Glackens, when the argument erupted over whether or not this item should be shown, the society's president solved the problem in one fell swoop: "Nobody noticed W[illiam] G[lackens] leave the group and quietly make his way to a corner where the disputed *objet d'art* sat on a floor beside a screen. He picked it up, held it over the screen, and dropped it. There was a crash. Everyone looked around startled. 'It broke!' he exclaimed".[9]

Of course, much gets distorted in the retelling of a story, but it is easy to imagine something like this having occurred at the SIA exhibition, and quite possibly not to the chamber pot he described, but to R. Mutt's *Fountain*. Saying that it "sat on a floor beside a screen" corroborates both the recollections of Duchamp and Theresa Bernstein, but if it was the Duchamp urinal he smashed, then it could not have gone to Stieglitz's gallery three days later. What could have happened—although there is no extant evidence to support this theory—is that after the photograph was taken, "Duchamp & Co.," as Stieglitz described them, retrieved the urinal from his gallery and brought it back to the Grand Central Palace, placing it in the same position where it had been displayed earlier—behind a partition or screen—since the exhibition did not close until May 6, 1917. It might have been at that point—when the urinal reappeared—that Glackens had had enough, and decided to settle the matter once and for all by smashing it to pieces. What is most convincing about this scenario is that we would have to imagine a motive that caused Glackens to make up this story, which Ira Glackens tells us that in the telling, Prendergast "laughed so hard" that "tears ran down his cheeks."[10]

No matter what accounts for the disappearance of the urinal, the very fact that an object of this importance and magnitude—one that contributed to changing the very definition of art—no longer exists today is an integral component of its mystique and allure. Just as with celebrities and world leaders who die before their time, we can only wonder what would have happened if the original artifact had survived. Would it be enshrined in a museum with visitors crowding in to see it, like tourists in the Louvre crowding before the *Mona Lisa*? Unlikely. It is not necessary to stand in front of a readymade to understand its meaning and importance; replicas, examples in edition and, for that matter, even reproductions in books can serve to stir the mind as intensely as the debate that occurred at the opening of the first SIA exhibition. What assures the historical longevity of *Fountain* is not the object itself, but those who think about its implications today, first and foremost artists who work in diverse styles and media, yet continue to be inspired by Duchamp and the ideas his work introduced a hundred years ago.

Mike Bidlo's *Fractured Fountain* (pl. 6) inspired the writing of this essay. During its display in an exhibition at my gallery in 2016, I began to contemplate the reasons Bidlo had so laboriously handcrafted a urinal in porcelain to match the design of the model used by Duchamp, only to then smash and glue the pieces together, later arranging for

**HIS ART TOO CRUDE FOR INDEPENDENTS**

**Mr. Mutt Thought He Could Exhibit Almost Anything, but the Society Thought Differently.**

You may call him what you will, a conservative is a conservative still—and Marcel Duchamp knows it. Therefore, the painter of "Nude Descending a Staircase" fame has declared his independence of the Independent Society of Artists, and there is dissension in the ranks of the organization that is holding at the Grand Central Palace the greatest exhibition of painting and sculpture in the history of the country.

It all grew out of the philosophy of J. C. Mutt, of Philadelphia, hitherto little known in artistic circles. When Mr. Mutt heard that payment of five dollars would permit him to send to the exhibition a work of art of any description or degree of excellence he might see fit he complied by shipping from the Quaker City a familiar article of bathroom furniture manufactured by a well known firm of that town. By the same mail went a five dollar bill.

To-day Mr Mutt has his exhibit and his $5; Mr. Duchamp has a headache, and the Society of Independent Artists has the resignation of one of its directors and a bad disposition.

After a long battle that lasted up to the opening hour of the exhibition, Mr. Mutt's defenders were voted down by a small margin. "The Fountain," as his entry was known, will never become an attraction—or detraction—of the improvised galleries of the Grand Central Palace, even if Mr. Duchamp goes to the length of withdrawing his own entry, "Tulip Hysteria Co-ordinating," in retaliation. "The Fountain," said the majority, "may be a very useful object in its place, but its place is not an art exhibition, and it is, by no definition, a work of art."

Fig. 3. "His Art Too Crude for Independents," *The New York Herald*, April 11, 1917 the reassembled work to be cast in bronze. Was it because he wanted to establish a rapport with Duchamp's *Large Glass*—which was also smashed and reassembled—or did he want us to reconsider what happened to the original *Fountain*? It is an example of how the work of a contemporary artist can affect our understanding of an event that took place in the distant past, in this case, one so momentous that it changed the future of art and the history of aesthetics.

[1] Beatrice Wood, *I Shock Myself* (San Francisco: Chronicle Books, 2006), p. 29. In earlier published accounts of this incident, Wood wrote that this argument took place with Rockwell Kent; see Francis M. Naumann, ed., "I Shock Myself: Excerpts from the Autobiography of Beatrice Wood," *Arts* 51, no. 9 (May 1977): pp. 135–36. With Marcel Duchamp and George Bellows, Kent served on the exhibition's hanging committee, and he was also in charge of the installation.

[2] "His Art Too Crude for Independents," *The New York Herald*, April 11, 1917: p. 6. I was the first to have discovered this article and quoted it in an essay on the exhibition: Francis M. Naumann, "The Big Show: The First Exhibition of the Society of Independent Artists, Part I," *Artforum* 17, no. 6 (February 1979): p. 38. Because of a scratch in the microfilm, I mistakenly read the date of this article as April 14, 1917 (instead of April 11, 1917), an error drawn to my attention by Bradley Bailey. Unfortunately, many scholars have quoted from this publication, so the date is given incorrectly in countless subsequent accounts of the incident and its aftermath.

[3] Pierre Cabanne, *Dialogues with Marcel Duchamp*, trans. Ron Padgett (New York: Viking Press, 1971), p. 55. The interviews took place in Paris in 1966, and were published for the first time in French, *Entretiens avec Marcel Duchamp* (Paris: Pierre Belfond, 1967).

[4] From an interview that I conducted with Theresa Bernstein at her home and studio in New York, April 29, 1989.

[5] Interview conducted at the Sidney Janis Gallery, New York, during the time of the Dada exhibition there in 1953 (unpublished; transcription provided by Carroll Janis, p. 43).

[6] Stieglitz to McBride, April 19, 1917, Henry McBride Papers, Yale Collection of American Literature, Beinecke Rare Book and Manuscript Library, Yale University, New Haven, CT. See also the diary of Beatrice Wood, entry for April 13, 1917, Archives of American Art, Smithsonian Institution, Washington, DC.

[7] Janis interview, transcription, p. 45 (emphasis added). It is likely that Duchamp is describing the first of these two photographs (fig. 1), as the Janis interview took place with a valise serving as a guide to generate questions, and a detail of that particular studio interior is reproduced there. It should be noted that this image was not used in the valise as an illustration for *Fountain* (for that was replicated three-dimensionally in another part of assembly), but as a reproduction of his *Hat Rack*, which is dated 1917 (and thus should not be used as an indication of the year when the photograph was taken).

[8] Duchamp to Roché, August 11, 1918, Henri-Pierre Roché Papers, Carlton Lake Collection of French Manuscripts, Harry Ransom Humanities Research Center, University of Texas, Austin, TX; published in Scarlett and Philippe Reliquet, eds., *Correspondance Marcel Duchamp – Henri-Pierre Roché 1918-1959* (Geneva: Mamco, 2012), pp. 15–16.

[9] Ira Glackens, *William Glackens and the Ashcan Group* (New York: Crown, 1957), p. 188.

[10] Glackens, *William Glackens and the Ashcan Group*, p. 187. Of course, if this scenario were accepted, it would mean that the urinal never returned to Duchamp's studio after having been sent to the SIA exhibition, so the photographs that show it hanging from a doorway (figs. 1, 2) would have to have been taken prior, that is to say, before April 1917. There is also the possibility that when the urinal never returned from the SIA exhibition, Duchamp acquired another and hung it in his studio, although there is no evidence to support such a hypothesis.

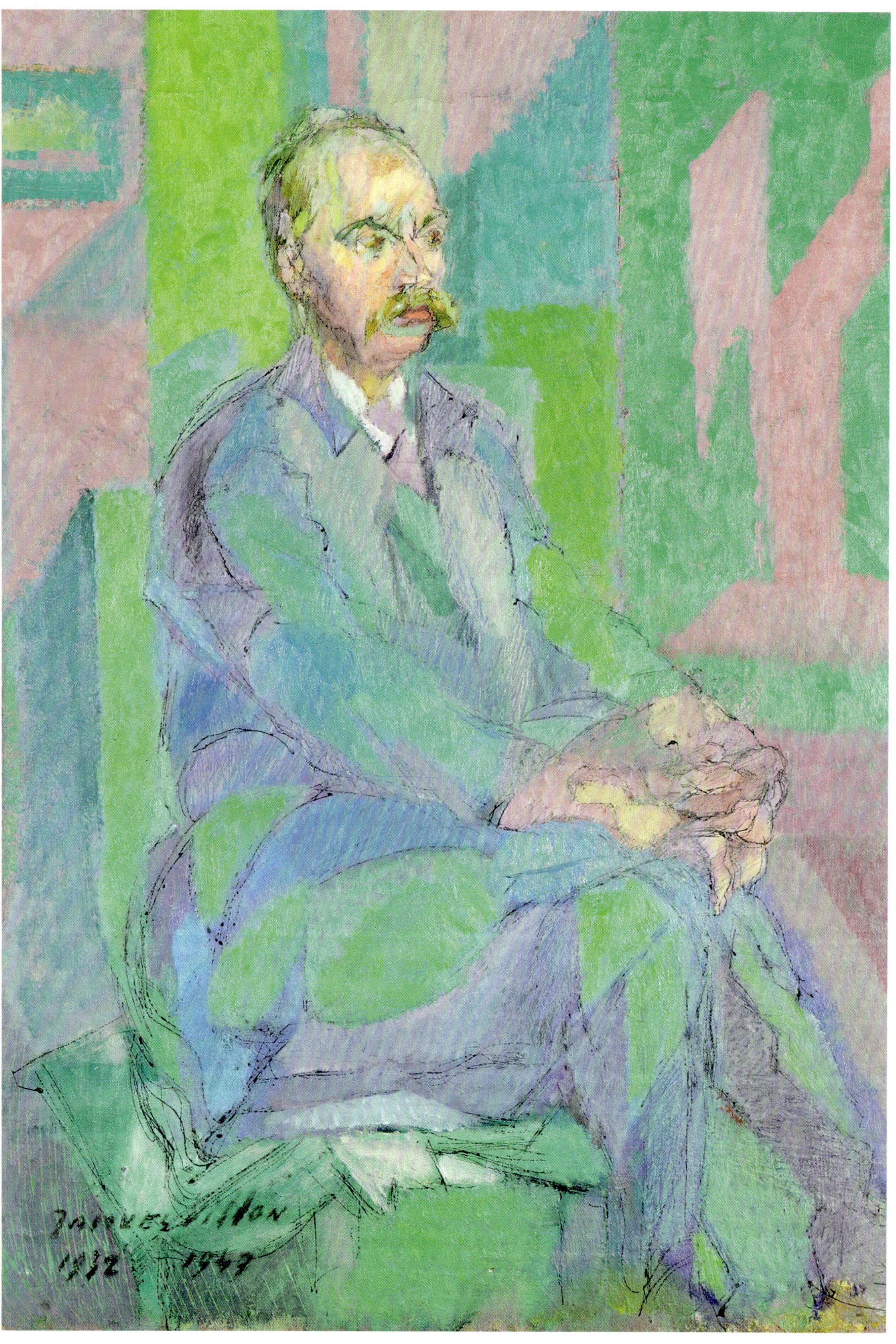
Jacques Villon
1932 1949

*Laurette E. McCarthy*

# Marcel Duchamp, Walter Pach, and the Urinal

The essential link between the inclusion of Marcel Duchamp's *Nude Descending a Staircase, No. 2* in the 1913 Armory Show, his arrival in New York in 1915 and introduction to Louise and Walter Arensberg, and the 1917 Society of Independent Artists' (SIA) inaugural exhibition—and therefore Duchamp's infamous/famous urinal—is American artist, critic, agent, historian, and impresario Walter Pach (fig. 4).[1] Pach was one of the most influential figures in the history of modern, American, and Mexican art about who little has been written; he was the subject of my dissertation and my biography of him, *Walter Pach (1883–1958): The Armory Show and the Untold Story of Modern Art in America*, was published in 2011.[2] Born and raised in New York City, Pach was the son of an upper middle-class family with his father's and uncles' photography company, Pach Brothers Studio, being the premier photographic firm in Manhattan with clients including the Metropolitan Museum of Art. Before he graduated from the College of the City of New York (CCNY), in 1903, Pach decided to pursue a career as an artist. He lived in Paris from the autumn of 1907 to the spring of 1908 and again from the fall of 1910 until the Armory Show opened in February 1913 and while there, Pach—who was fluent in German, French, Italian, and Spanish, spoke some Dutch and read a little Japanese—became a true insider in the contemporary art scene. He developed friendships with numerous European artists but became especially close with the Duchamp brothers: Jacques Villon, Raymond Duchamp-Villon, and Marcel Duchamp; he named his only child after Raymond. His attention was drawn to Duchamp-Villon's sculpture through another friend, American art collector Michael Stein, brother of Leo and Gertrude Stein.[3]

Fig. 4. Jacques Villon
(French; 1875–1963)
*Portrait of Walter Pach*,
1932–47
Oil on canvas
21 ¾ x 18 ¼ inches
The Minneapolis Institute of Arts, The John R. Van Derlip Fund

Photo: Minneapolis Institute of Art

Beginning around 1911, the Duchamp brothers' shared studio in Puteaux, a suburb of Paris, became a gathering place on Sundays for painters and sculptors including Francis Picabia, Jean Metzinger, Fernand Léger, Robert Delaunay, Marie Laurencin, and André Mare (fig. 5). This group also met on Mondays at the home of fellow painter Albert Gleizes in nearby Courbevoie. These artists were joined by poets and writers such as Alexandre Mercereau, Guillaume Apollinaire, Roger Allard, and André Salmon.[4] Pach was the only American artist and critic to be part of this group and friends with Marcel Duchamp at this time.[5]

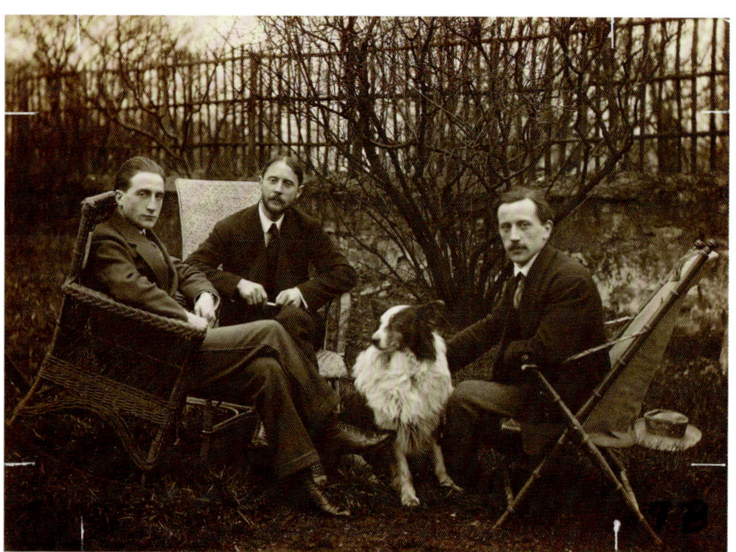

Fig. 5. *Marcel Duchamp, Jacques Villon, and Raymond Duchamp-Villon, in the garden of Villon's studio, Puteaux, France*, ca. 1913
Walt Kuhn, Kuhn family papers, and Armory Show records, Archives of American Art, Smithsonian Institution, Washington, DC

Between 1910 and 1912, he undoubtedly saw works by Duchamp at the Puteaux studio and in the various Parisian Salons. It was, however, the presentation of six of Duchamp's paintings at the fall 1912 *Salon de la Section d'Or* exhibition that particularly struck him.[6]

The Section d'Or exhibition served as one basis for Pach's selection of works for the 1913 Armory Show and from this display he personally picked four of Duchamp's works, including *Nude Descending a Staircase, No. 2*. While credit has usually been given to Arthur B. Davies and Walt Kuhn for the selection of European works for this groundbreaking show, Pach was actually the curator of the stylistically vanguard European, and predominately Parisian-based, section of the Armory Show. It was Pach who made the final selection of virtually all of the works sent from Europe.[7] Later in life Duchamp explained how he came to be invited to the Armory Show: "By Walter Pach. He had come to France in 1910, and he had made friends with my brothers, through whom we met. Then in 1912, when he was entrusted with the task of gathering paintings for that show, he saved a lot of room for the three of us. . . . He took four of my things: the 'Nude Descending a Staircase,' the 'Young Man,' the 'Portrait of Chess Players,' and 'The King and Queen Surrounded by Swift Nudes'."[8]

Pach also traveled to the United States from Paris for the Armory Show and among the multiple roles he played during the entire, three-city run of the exhibition was chief sales agent.[9] He kept two small notebooks in which he recorded every sale.[10] It was Pach who brokered the sale of all four of Duchamp's paintings at the Armory Show. The *Nude Descending a Staircase, No. 2* was bought by San Francisco dealer Frederic C. Torrey who had come to see the show in New York but apparently could not wait until he got home to buy the painting. He got off the train in Albuquerque, New Mexico, and sent a cable to Pach on March 1, 1913 to purchase the work.[11] Pach recorded the sale in his record book on March 5th (fig. 6).[12] Six years later, in 1919, when Torrey wanted to sell the painting he contacted Pach who, eventually, sold it to Walter Arensberg.[13] Duchamp's *The Chess Players* and *The King and Queen Surrounded by Swift Nudes* were acquired by Chicago lawyer Arthur Jerome Eddy on March 1st and 2nd at the New York venue of the show, again through Pach, and these works too were eventually purchased by the Arensbergs.[14] The fourth of Duchamp's paintings, *Sad Young Man on a Train*, was sold by Pach to Chicago painter and architectural draftsman Manierre Dawson at the Chicago venue of the Armory Show.[15] In 1922, Dawson sold this painting to Pach who in turn sold it to Peggy Guggenheim in 1942; it is now located in the Peggy Guggenheim Collection in Venice.[16] Duchamp heard about the sales of his works from the Armory Show through letters that Pach sent to his brothers and he wrote Pach on July 2, 1913: "I have heard through my brothers all the good news regarding the exhibition in America. I am very happy; and I thank you for the dedication with which you have defended our painting." In the same letter Duchamp also noted: "The weather is very nice at Puteaux on Sundays, and you must miss taking part in our games in the garden. Will you be back with us soon? Don't you miss Paris a little," giving a glimpse into the closeness of their friendship and their days together in Paris.[17]

The Armory Show generated tremendous interest in stylistically vanguard painting and sculpture in the United States, especially in New York, and before the exhibition closed several galleries there began to show this type of art. Pach became the European representative for three of them: Montross, Carroll, and Bourgeois. He served as the intermediary between these dealers and artists including Marcel Duchamp. In the fall of 1914, soon after World War I broke out, Pach un-

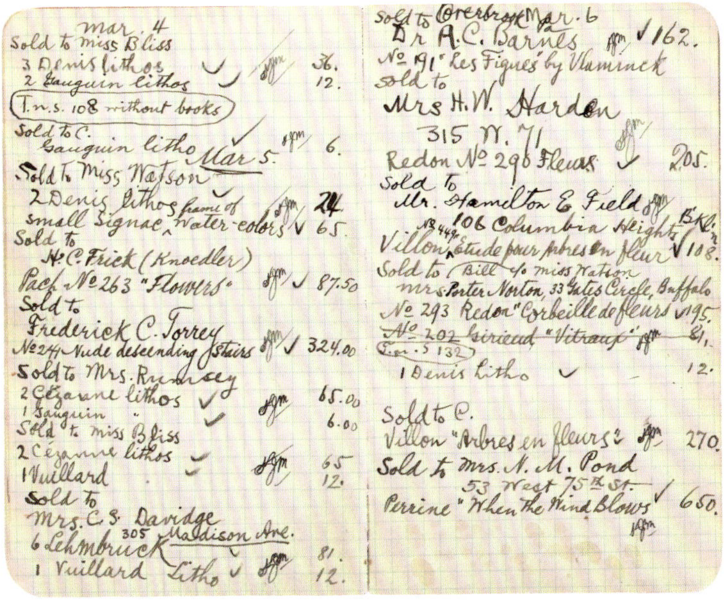

Fig. 6. Walter Pach's Red Record Book of Sales Walter Pach Papers, 1857–1980, Archives of American Art, Smithsonian Institution, Washington, DC

dertook the dangerous wartime journey to Paris determined to acquire as many works as possible from friends and colleagues for exhibitions in New York.[18] From late 1914 until 1916, he acted on Duchamp's behalf in Manhattan, placing his works in shows and brokering sales of his art to private collectors.[19]

Duchamp's decision to come to the United States in 1915 was a direct result of his friendship with Pach; he knew no-one else in the country. In April 1915, Duchamp wrote Pach: "I have absolutely decided to leave France" and swore his friend to secrecy as he had not broached the subject with his family yet.[20] In another letter he told Pach: "If you remember our talks on the Boulevards St. Michel and Raspail, you will see my intentions to depart as a necessary consequence of these conversations. *I do not go to New York I leave Paris*. It is altogether different . . . I beg you not to believe that my brothers think you might be pressuring me. The three of us have too much confidence and friendship for you. I am sure they will find at least some comfort in knowing that I will be there with you."[21] The content and tone of these letters reveal the intimacy of this friendship and the candor with which the two men communicated and the mention of "our talks" undoubtedly refers to conversations between the two when Pach was in Paris in the fall of 1914.

After receiving Duchamp's April letters, Pach wrote New York lawyer and modern art collector John Quinn that Duchamp was "one of the finest young men I know, with one of the most brilliant minds."[22] Walter Pach was really the first critic, American or European, to recognize Duchamp's genius. Writing about an early work by Duchamp, he recalled "Duchamp-Villon's showing me a study by Marcel that marked a big new departure. We looked at it, Villon and I, and we said, 'You are going pretty far.' He was; he was going to cross the line that marks the separation between painting done from nature, or even derived from nature, and painting whose forms are neither imitated nor remembered nor yet adapted: for once a man was going to create his own image, which is to say that of the mind."[23]

Since Duchamp was determined to come to New York, Pach happily and graciously assisted him in every way possible. As noted Duchamp scholar Francis M. Naumann observed: "aboard ship, it was Pach's address that Duchamp listed as his destination in America."[24] When Duchamp arrived in New York in June 1915, it was Pach who met him at the dock and took him into his home and soon thereafter painted a portrait of him.[25] In one of his April 1915 letters to Pach, Duchamp had written that he wanted to come to the United States, "But only *on the condition* that I could earn my living there."[26] Pach obliged by introducing Duchamp to the director of the Institut Français where the young Frenchman did indeed get a job so he could earn his living.[27] Duchamp's presence in New York was met with great interest by the press who interviewed him several times after he arrived, as he was still famous from his scandalous *Nude Descending a Staircase, No. 2*

Fig. 7. "Marcel Duchamp Visits New York," *Vanity Fair* (September 1915): p. 57

## MARCEL DUCHAMP VISITS NEW YORK

MARCEL DUCHAMP has arrived in New York!

You don't know him? Impossible! Why, he painted the "Nude Descending a Staircase," a painting which made such a turmoil here a couple of years ago.

It is safe to say that no other painting ever caused such a furore. It was the one thing that was not missed by any of the hundred thousand odd persons who visited the International Exhibition at the Armory, or the two hundred thousand who went to the same show at the Chicago Art Institute, or the sixty thousand who flocked to the Copley Society Gallery in Boston. How many have seen it since it found a happy home in San Francisco, it is impossible to say.

It was discussed at dinner parties, at dances, in boxes at the opera, in editorials, and by the writers of so called "witty paragraphs." It caused more disputes than politics. Every humorist among the illustrators took a whack at it, and it was reproduced in newspapers in every city of the United States.

If you said you understood what the artist was driving at, some of your friends said that you were an affected humbug; if you said that you didn't, others of your friends said that you were stupid. Mr. W. M. Chase laughed loud and long before it. Mr. Kenyon Cox was surprised and shocked, and most of the members of the National Academy shook their heads sadly. To one critic it suggested an explosion in a lumber mill. Another professed to have discovered the figure of the nude—which wasn't there, for the painting is a story in motion, that and nothing more. Anyhow it was, as Southey might have said, a famous victory—for M. Marcel Duchamp.

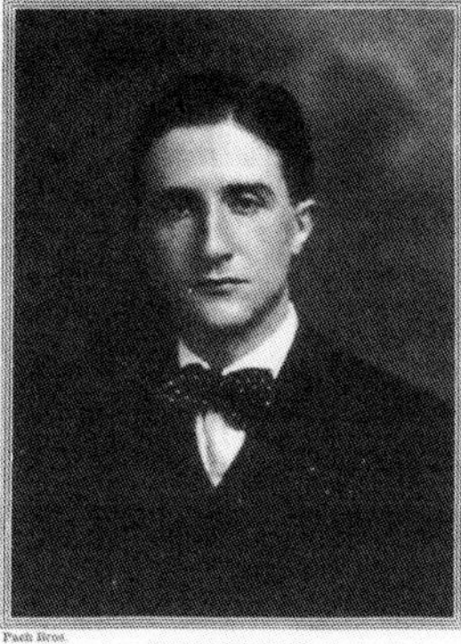

Pach Bros.

MARCEL DUCHAMP

*who became famous because of his "Nude Descending a Staircase," and who is now in New York*

Marcel Duchamp would be at the front, fighting for France, but the doctors wouldn't let him go. His immediate family is well represented by his brothers Raymond Duchamp-Villon, the architect and sculptor, and Jacques Villon a painter like himself. He is only twenty-eight. He speaks English like an Englishman; has an insatiable curiosity about everything in New York, from Coney Island to the Metropolitan Museum; is completely without affectation and is much more interested in hearing the opinions of other people than in expressing his own.

Marcel Duchamp is not going to play while here. He is anxious to see what ideas America—a great new experience—will supply; ideas that may be expressed in his work. His standing in French art is secure. As far back as 1910 he was recognized as a leader of the advanced men, and was elected a member of the Society which gives the exhibition commonly known as the Salon d'Automne.

WHEN you ask him if he is a Cubist, or a This, or a That, he says simply that he is a painter, trying to express his ideas in his own way. The tags and definitions, and names of schools, have, he says, all been invented and applied by outsiders, and the poor artists are not to be blamed if they are card indexed and thrust into pigeonholes by those who talk about them.

from two years earlier, and the photograph provided for *Vanity Fair*'s September 1915 article was taken by none other than Gotthelf Pach, Walter's father (fig. 7).[28] A few weeks after Duchamp arrived, Pach arranged for him to stay at the apartment of his friends Louise and Walter Arensberg at 33 West 67th Street and later introduced him to the couple.[29]

By 1916, Duchamp was firmly ensconced in the New York art scene thanks, in very large part, to the efforts of his dear friend Walter Pach. During that summer and fall a group of artists, writers, and musicians—which included French émigrés Duchamp, Jean Crotti, Albert Gleizes, and Francis Picabia, as well as Americans Pach, Joseph Stella, Charles Sheeler, Morton L. Schamberg, John Covert, Katherine S. Dreier, and poet Wallace Stevens—gathered at the Arensbergs' apartment to discuss the founding of the American version of the Société des Artistes Indépendants.[30] Pach was quite close with the French artists, having met all of them in Paris between 1910 and early 1912, and it was most likely Pach who introduced his friends Stella, Sheeler, and Schamberg to this group as well. While the number of contemporary art exhibitions in New York had increased since the Armory Show, the group that gathered at the Arensbergs' felt there was a need for a more formal annual exhibition which would, "bring together the public and the artists who felt the vital movement of the time."[31] According to an unsigned manuscript in the SIA archives, "The Independents was really organized by Walter Pach, with the advice of Albert Gleizes and Marcel Duchamp who were in this country, and the encouragement of Morton L. Schamberg."[32] This view was corroborated by Helen Farr Sloan in two interviews in which she noted that Pach was indeed the prime mover behind the founding of the SIA and was its driving force from its inception to its close in 1944.[33]

The SIA adopted the "No Jury, No Prizes" motto of its French forebear and its primary purpose was to hold a yearly exhibition that was completely free from the constraints of the established jury and prize system of the old-guard New York art world.[34] The directors began planning the first show in the fall of 1916 and Pach was involved with every stage of the operations; Duchamp was no doubt fully aware of Pach's multiple and multifaceted roles in the undertaking. Early in 1917, Pach drafted the circular sent by the SIA to painters, sculptors, and the press which announced the spring show "in which all artists may participate independently of the decisions of juries."[35] The response was overwhelming and Pach wrote art critic Henry McBride: "Applications are simply pouring in and the success of the show is certain. Also I believe we shall do what we most want: reach the kind of people who have no chance to show otherwise."[36] He also told Quinn: "In two weeks over six hundred applications have come in. We are going to have a good many of the known men and, I believe, some worthwhile stuff from the unknown men. That is what I am interested in."[37] The open door policy of the SIA encouraged all artists to participate and while the directors, and more particularly Pach, understood that the quality of art submitted would be uneven, they were convinced that the opportunities provided by the SIA shows were vital for the future of art in America.

The "No Jury" tenet upon which the society was founded was tested before the first show opened by the submission of a porcelain urinal signed "R. Mutt." Numerous accounts of the circumstances surrounding this incident have been published, discussed, and repeated; however, none of them really address Walter Pach's role in this divisive event.[38] This oversight is quite shocking considering that the reason Duchamp was in New York in the first place was because of his friendship with Pach. In addition, it was the latter who introduced Duchamp to the group that formed the SIA and, as mentioned, Duchamp helped Pach formulate the organization. There are, in fact, published and unpublished references to Pach's relation to this episode that shed intriguing and important light on the circumstances surrounding Duchamp's urinal.

One of the most interesting, and arguably telling, of these accounts of Pach's involvement with the urinal was by noted printmaker, dealer, and curator Carl Zigrosser who was quite close with Pach and who first met Duchamp through him.[39] Later in life, Zigrosser wrote: "Marcel Duchamp was the enfant terrible of modern art, the Dad of Dada, and the Grandpappy of Pop. He achieved notoriety in America at the Armory Show and also perpetrated some of the most sardonic spoofs or hoaxes ever made in art history, from the 'urinal affair' to his final legacy."[40] Of his acquaintance with Duchamp, Zigrosser said that he first met him through Pach and wrote: "It must have occurred before Duchamp's prank with the Society of Independent Artists, which seemed to me to have been designed especially to get Walter's goat. Walter Pach, who was very earnest and ponderous about 'art' and also very proper about morals, was an officer of the Society, which had been founded to provide exhibition facilities to anyone, without restriction or censorship. Marcel submitted a porcelain urinal as a piece of sculpture under the pseudonym of 'R. Mutt' for exhibition in the Annual. He thereby put to test the Society's slogan of no censorship, and created a scandal that almost broke up the Society. The piece was rejected, and some of the executive board resigned."[41] Zigrosser's view of Duchamp's urinal submission as a practical joke specifically aimed at Walter Pach raises questions about current interpretations of the work and, perhaps, suggests new ways of engaging the object and discussing it.

In another tale of events, William Mills Ivins, Jr., who was appointed the curator of prints at the Metropolitan Museum of Art in 1916, the year the SIA was founded, wrote about the gatherings at the Arensbergs' apartment that "Walter Pach for a while came quite regularly but he had his celebrated falling down or out with Duchamp and as Duchamp was there all the time Walter Pach rather faded away."[42] This argument between Pach and Duchamp could only have been caused by the urinal and Pach's response to it; Pach probably knew that it was submitted by Duchamp. The rift between these two close friends, which was very personal and quite traumatic, lasted over a year and caused quite a strain on Marcel's brothers, especially Raymond with whom Pach was particularly close. In May 1918, Raymond responded to a letter from Pach saying: "I am really glad the estrangement period between Marcel and you is over. I was sure it wouldn't last, but suffered from it. Marcel's last letter fully reassures me from this point of view. I'm thinking of writing him soon so please let him know this when you say a word for me."[43] It is clear from these primary and secondary sources that Pach was at the very center of the controversy surrounding the urinal and his years-long friendship with Duchamp was significantly damaged because of his vote to dismiss the work from the exhibition.

In 1922, five years after the incident of the urinal, there was another "squabble" among the ranks of the SIA with Pach at the center and the published arguments reflected back to 1917 and Pach's role in that divisive episode. This time renowned French-American sculptor Gaston Lachaise, who was also friends with Duchamp, resigned from the SIA amid accusations that Pach was favoring his friends through advanced publicity for the exhibition.[44] Artist, critic, editor, and dealer Hamilton Easter Field lodged his complaints in the pages of *The Arts* magazine writing: "Lachaise's resignation is but one event in a long series all showing how much Pach is distrusted by those who come into contact with him. From the time of the first Independent Show, when Joseph Stella, Walter Arensberg, Duchamps [sic], and others resigned, there has been the same distrust . . . Until Walter Pach and his methods are eliminated we shall continue to have such scandals as the one which caused the wholesale resignations the first year and that which now has caused the resignation of Gaston Lachaise."[45] Clearly Field felt that Pach was almost solely to blame for the repression of the urinal and the resignations of Duchamp and others from the SIA in 1917. Painter John Sloan, president of the SIA and a very close friend of Pach, thought that Field's attack on Pach was "entirely unwarranted and based on personal animus" and he, as well as numerous others associated with the SIA, supported Pach's role within the organization from its inception in 1917 and throughout its existence.[46]

In 1936, Pach weighed in on this divisive event in response to publications by Alfred H. Barr, Jr. for his show *Fantastic Art, Dada and Surrealism* at the Museum of Modern Art. As Francis M. Naumann first noted, while the official letter sent to Barr was typed and signed by John Sloan, the original letter was handwritten by Pach and in it he describes his version of the circumstances surrounding the 1917 SIA exhibition and Duchamp's urinal which read, in part:

> The bulletin says, "In the first New York Independent's exhibition, 1917, he [Duchamp] entered a porcelain toilet accessory with the title *Fontaine* and signed it R. Mutt in order to test the impartiality of the jury of which he was himself a member."
> The catalogue says, "1917 Duchamp sent a 'ready-made' to the Independents, a porcelain plumbing fixture which he called 'Fontaine' and signed R. Mutt: rejected by the jury from which he resigned."
> Our Society, like the French society whose principles and practice it continues, has never had a jury, and to treat the exclusion of the exhibit signed R. Mutt as the action of a jury is to misrepresent the work carried on for over fifty years in France and America by artists who have conscientiously adhered to the idea on which these societies are based: No Jury, No Prizes.
> Every exhibition must have some sort of executive committee and the by-laws of our Society . . . clearly state the administrative duties of the directors. . . . Their function in every case is distinct from that of a jury, which is a body that passes on aesthetic merits. On occasions when we have exceeded what the police thought to be our rights, we have been brought into court and subjected to fine or imprisonment for "outraging public decency."
> It was to avoid difficulties of such a nature that the exclusion of 1917 was voted . . . Mr. Duchamp was as free to exhibit his "ready-mades" as he had been the year previous, in a show composed largely of members of

> our Board of 1917; he could not, as we felt, be permitted to place in the exhibition an object which by its nature would have aroused such disgust and resentment among the members and visitors of the Society as to endanger the continuance of the work which had been undertaken and has been carried on ever since. Therefore, when you say we had a jury and when, further, you make mention of "impartiality," we consider that you are so far from the truth of the matter as to render it proper that you correct the statements referred to, and do so as publicly as they were made . . .
>
> By covering up under inoffensive words the whole question we had to face, you change the issue and put us in the position of rejecting an exhibit offered as a work of art when, as you must know, we were dealing with a matter totally unrelated with art.[47]

It seems clear from these numerous references that Duchamp's selection and submission of a urinal to the 1917 show of the SIA, its subsequent refusal to be exhibited, and the resignation of Duchamp and others from the board were all directly connected to Walter Pach. From the latter's point of view, both at the time of the show and twenty years later, Duchamp's urinal was not excluded based upon aesthetic or artistic merits, which he viewed as the province of a jury; rather, as Pach argued, the committee ruled against its inclusion in the show because of the effect its presence could have had on the very existence of the SIA. With the future of the organization at stake, Pach took his stand against the urinal, a decision that deeply damaged a dear friendship.

If not for Walter Pach, Marcel Duchamp's *Nude Descending a Staircase, No. 2* would not have been included in the 1913 Armory Show and Duchamp never would have journeyed to New York in 1915, met the Arensbergs, and helped formulate the Society of Independent Artists. Evidence also suggests that Pach may well have been the spark that ignited Duchamp's submission of a porcelain urinal to the SIA, triggering a debate and discussion that resonates to this very day. One could conjecture, then, that without Walter Pach the trajectory of Marcel Duchamp's artistic career in the United States and, arguably, the development of modern and contemporary art in general could/would have been markedly different.

[1] I want to thank Francis M. Naumann for his groundbreaking research work and publications on the relationship between Marcel Duchamp and Walter Pach. For Pach's relationship with Marcel Duchamp, see: Walter Pach, *Queer Thing, Painting: Forty Years in the World of Art* (New York: Harper & Brothers, 1938), chapter 11; Francis M. Naumann, "Amicalement, Marcel: Fourteen Letters from Marcel Duchamp to Walter Pach," *Archives of American Art Journal* 29, no. 3-4 (1989): pp. 36–50, and *New York Dada, 1915–23* (New York: Harry N. Abrams Inc., 1994), pp. 25–28 and 34–37; and Laurette E. McCarthy, *Walter Pach (1883–1958): The Armory Show and the Untold Story of Modern Art in America* (University Park: The Pennsylvania State University Press, 2011) chapters 3, 6, and 7. The original of all of Duchamp's letters to Pach are housed in the Walter Pach Papers, Archives of American Art (AAA), 1857–1980, Smithsonian Institution, Washington, DC (hereinafter Pach Papers).

[2] Laurette E. McCarthy, "Walter Pach: Artist, Critic, Historian, and Agent of Modernism," Ph.D., University of Delaware, 1996, and *Walter Pach (1883–1958)*, 2011.

[3] Walter Pach, *A Sculptor's Architecture* (New York: Association of American Painters and Sculptors, 1913), p. 9, and *Queer Thing, Painting*, pp. 142–43; and Judith K. Zilczer, "Raymond Duchamp-Villon and the American Avant-Garde," *Archives of American Art Journal* 38, no. 1-2 (1998): p. 15.

[4] Judith K. Zilczer, "Raymond Duchamp-Villon: Pioneer of Modern Sculpture," *Philadelphia Museum of Art Bulletin* 76 (Fall 1980): pp. 3–4.

[5] For discussions of Pach's affiliation with the Puteaux Group see: Pach, *Queer Thing, Painting*, pp. 139–63; McCarthy, *Walter Pach (1883–1958)*, chapter 3; Allan Antliff, *Anarchist Modernism: Art, Politics, and the First American Avant-Garde* (Chicago and London: University of Chicago Press), pp. 167 and 172–82; and Mark Antliff, *Inventing Bergson: Cultural Politics and the Parisian Avant-Garde* (Princeton, NJ: Princeton University Press, 1993), p. 39.

[6] Pach, *Queer Thing, Painting*, p. 156 and Naumann, "Amicalement, Marcel: Fourteen Letters from Marcel Duchamp to Walter Pach," p. 36.

[7] For Pach's involvement in the Armory Show see: Laurette E. McCarthy, "The 'Truths' About the Armory Show: Walter Pach's Side of the Story," *Archives of American Art Journal* 44, no. 3-4 (2004): pp. 2–13; *Walter Pach (1883–1958)*, chapter 3; "Armory Show: New Perspectives and Recent Rediscoveries," *Archives of American Art Journal* 51, no. 3-4 (Winter 2012): pp. 22–35; "Walter Pach: Agent of Modernism," in *The Armory Show at 100: Modernism and Revolution* (New York: New-York Historical Society, 2013).

[8] Pierre Cabanne, *Dialogues with Marcel Duchamp*, trans. Ron Pladget (New York: Viking Press, 1971), pp. 43–44.

[9] See note 7.

[10] Walter Pach's Red Record Book of Sales and Brown Record Book of Sales, Pach Papers. Francis M. Naumann rediscovered these very important materials in 2011 and graciously donated them to the AAA.

[11] Telegram from Frederic C. Torrey to Walter Pach, March 1, 1913, Elmer L. MacRae Papers, Collection Archives, Hirshhorn Museum and Sculpture Garden, Smithsonian Institution, Washington, DC. See also Francis M. Naumann, "Frederic C. Torrey and Duchamp's *Nude Descending a Staircase*," in Bonnie Clearwater, ed., *West Coast Duchamp* (Miami Beach: Grassfield Press, 1991), pp. 11–13.

[12] Pach's Red Record Book of Sales, Pach Papers, "Mar. 5, Sold to Frederick [sic] C. Torrey No 241 Nude Descending Stairs 324.00."

[13] Naumann, "Frederic C. Torrey and Duchamp's *Nude Descending a Staircase*," p. 20 and McCarthy, *Walter Pach (1883–1958)*, pp. 92 and 188 notes 26 and 27.

[14] Pach's Red Record Book of Sales, Pach Papers, "Mar. 1 Sold to Mr. A.J. Eddy Duchamp's 'Joueurs d'Echecs' 162" and "Mar. 2 Sold to Mr. A.J Eddy No 239 Duchamp's 'Le Roi et la Reine' 324." See Calvin Tompkins, *Duchamp: A Biography* (New York: Henry Holt and Company, 1996), pp. 163 and 294.

[15] Pach's Brown Record Book of Sales, Pach Papers, "April 7 Sold to Mr. Dawson Duchamp's 'Nu-esquisse'," p. 162.

[16] McCarthy, *Walter Pach (1883–1958)*, p. 102 and Tompkins, *Duchamp: A Biography*, pp. 310–11.

[17] Marcel Duchamp to Walter Pach, July 2, 1913, in Naumann, "Amicalement, Marcel: Fourteen Letters from Marcel Duchamp to Walter Pach," p. 37.

[18] McCarthy, *Walter Pach (1883–1958)*, pp. 68–69.

[19] Naumann, "Amicalement, Marcel: Fourteen Letters from Marcel Duchamp to Walter Pach," pp. 37–42 and McCarthy, *Walter Pach (1883–1958)*, pp. 70–74.

[20] Duchamp to Pach, April 2, 1915, in Naumann, "Amicalement, Marcel: Fourteen Letters from Marcel Duchamp to Walter Pach," p. 39.

[21] Duchamp to Pach, April 27, 1915, in Naumann, "Amicalement, Marcel: Fourteen Letters from Marcel Duchamp to Walter Pach," p. 40.

[22] Walter Pach to John Quinn, April 15, 1915, John Quinn Collection, Archives of American Art, Reel 2017L; McCarthy, *Walter Pach (1883–1958)*, p. 90; and Bennard B. Perlman, ed., *American Artists, Authors, and Collectors: The Walter Pach Letters, 1906–1958* (Albany: State University of New York Press, 2002), pp. 252–53.

[23] Pach, *Queer Thing, Painting*, p. 158.

[24] Naumann, *New York Dada*, p. 36.

[25] Naumann, *New York Dada*, p. 36 and

"Amicalement, Marcel: Fourteen Letters from Marcel Duchamp to Walter Pach," pp. 48–49, note 30.

[26] Duchamp to Pach, April 2, 1915, in Naumann, "Amicalement, Marcel: Fourteen Letters from Marcel Duchamp to Walter Pach," p. 39.

[27] McCarthy, *Walter Pach (1883–1958)*, p. 90.

[28] "Marcel Duchamp Visits New York," *Vanity Fair* (September 1915): p. 57 and Naumann, *New York Dada*, pp. 35–36.

[29] For more on the Arensbergs and their collection see: Francis M. Naumann, "Walter Conrad Arensberg: Poet, Patron, and Participant in the New York Avant-Garde, 1915–20," pp. 3–33. For Pach and the Arensbergs see McCarthy, *Walter Pach (1883–1958)*, pp. 45, 49–50, and 87–95.

[30] For more on the gatherings at the Arensbergs' apartment see Naumann, *New York Dada*, pp. 22–33 and "Walter Conrad Arensberg: Poet, Patron, and Participant in the New York Avant-Garde, 1915–20," pp. 3–33. For a description of Pach's involvement with the SIA see McCarthy, *Walter Pach (1883–1958)*, chapter 7.

[31] Pach, *Queer Thing, Painting*, p. 231.

[32] Unsigned manuscript, Records of The Society of Independent Artists (Incorporated), John Sloan Collection, Helen Farr Sloan Library & Archives, Delaware Art Museum, Wilmington, DE (hereinafter SIA Records). For Duchamp's involvement see also Pach, *Queer Thing, Painting*, p. 231.

[33] Helen Farr Sloan, interview with the author, April 6, 1994, Wilmington, DE and Helen Farr Sloan, interview with Clark S. Marlor, Wilmington, DE, August 8, 1978. For the latter see Clark S. Marlor, *The Society of Independent Artists: The Exhibition Record, 1917–1944* (Park Ridge, NJ: Noyes Press, 1984), pp. 3 and 23, note 6.

[34] By-Laws of the Society of Independent Artists, unpaginated, SIA Records.

[35] Typescript of the foreword to the 1917 catalog on which is handwritten "Introduction to Catalogue-by Walter Pach," and "Foreword," *The Society of Independent Artists 1917 Exhibition Catalogue*, unpaginated, SIA Records.

[36] Walter Pach to Henry McBride, January 24, 1917, Henry McBride Papers, Yale Collection of American Literature, Beinecke Rare Book and Manuscript Library, Yale University, New Haven, CT.

[37] Pach to Quinn, January 30, 1917, Quinn Collection. Also quoted in Perlman, *American Artists, Authors, and Collectors*, p. 279.

[38] For an in-depth study concerning *Fountain* and its history see William A. Camfield, *Marcel Duchamp Fountain* (Houston: Houston Fine Art Press, 1989). For a full account of the first SIA show see Francis M. Naumann, "The Big Show: The First Exhibition of the Society of Independent Artists, Part I," *Artforum* 17, no. 6 (February 1979): pp. 34–39, and "The Big Show: The First Exhibition of the Society of Independent Artists, Part II: The Critical Response," *Artforum* 17, no. 8 (April 1979): pp. 49–53.

[39] Carl Zigrosser, *A World of Art and Museums* (Philadelphia and London: The Art Alliance Press and Associated University Presses, 1975), p. 179.

[40] Zigrosser, *A World of Art and Museums*, p. 179.

[41] Zigrosser, *A World of Art and Museums*, pp. 179–80.

[42] William Mills Ivins, Jr., to Fiske Kimball, March 15, 1954, William Ivins Papers, unmicrofilmed, box 1, f. Arensberg, Archives of American Art, Smithsonian Institution, Washington, DC.

[43] Raymond Duchamp-Villon to Walter Pach, May 20, 1918, Pach Papers, Reel 4217, frs. 408–409.

[44] "Artists Squabble on Eve of Show: Gaston Lachaise Resigns From Independents—Editor Blames Walter Pach, John Sloan Defends Him," *New York Times*, February 24, 1922.

[45] Hamilton Easter Field, "Comments on the Arts," *The Arts* 2 (January 1922): p. 234.

[46] "Artists Squabble on Eve of Show."

[47] Walter Pach to Alfred H. Barr, Jr., former director of the Museum of Modern Art in New York, undated, SIA Records. See also Naumann, "Amicalement, Marcel: Fourteen Letters from Marcel Duchamp to Walter Pach," p. 49, note 47.

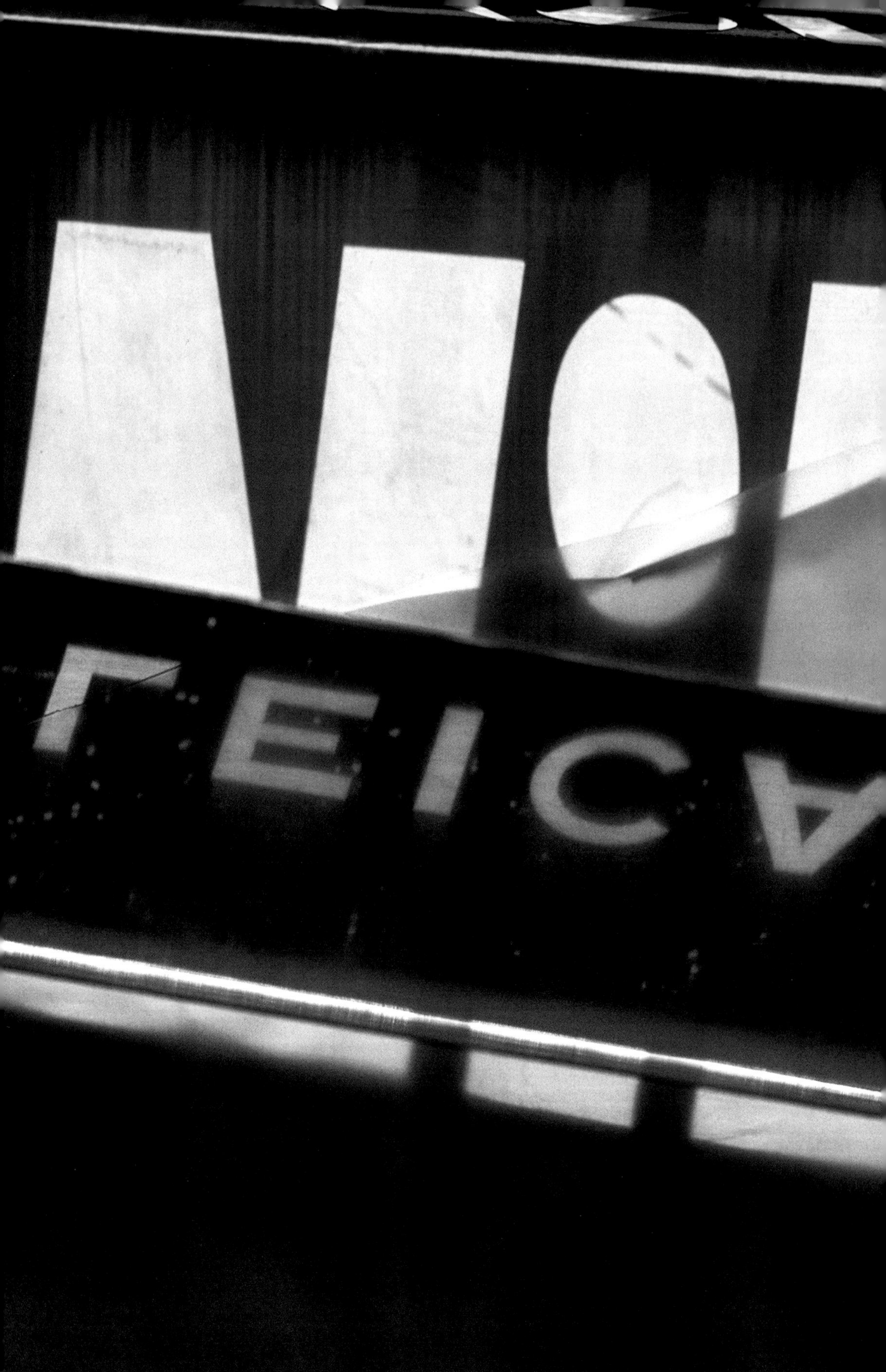
LEICA

*Bonnie Clearwater*

# Some Aesthetic Decisions

The first exhibition of the Society of Independent Artists (SIA), held in New York in April 1917, had 1,200 artists represented by 2,500 works.[1] But it is primarily known by the only work that was rejected by this unjuried exhibition—Marcel Duchamp's *Fountain*, 1917, a urinal signed "R. Mutt." Duchamp, a member of the organization's board, resigned after *Fountain* was rejected. He even quipped to his sister Suzanne that he intended to organize a special exhibition for "things refused at the Independents, but that would be a pleonasm! And the urinal would have been lonely."[2]

Duchamp contended that art was created out of "our urge for understanding."[3] For him, making art was an intellectual inquiry into the very nature of art. *Fountain* opened multiple avenues for inquiry, most significantly how Duchamp's act of choosing a found object and giving it a title, created a new "view point" and "new thought for it."[4] The present exhibition, *Some Aesthetic Decisions*, concentrates on the work of a selection of artists whose intellectual pursuits and questioning of the nature of art led them to make their own discoveries concerning aesthetics, value judgments, the relationship between the art work and the viewer, and the role reproduction plays in increasing or diminishing a work's aura. Although Duchamp moved permanently to New York during World War II, and participated in America's emerging art world, the full impact of his work was delayed until the late 1950s when it found a receptive audience in such artists as Robert Rauschenberg and Jasper Johns, composer John Cage and choreographer Merce Cunningham, who introduced it to a new generation of artists.[5]

Several artists in the exhibition respond to *Fountain* directly, starting with Alfred Stieglitz's photograph of Duchamp's original work, which was first published in the periodical *The Blind Man*, no. 2, May 1917 (pl. 1). Stieglitz, a major proponent of photography and modern art, was on the board of the SIA. Duchamp brought the work to Stieglitz's studio to be photographed, but it is likely that he left it to the photographer to choose how he would document it. Stieglitz transformed Duchamp's work into a signature work of his own by imposing his taste for sensuous form and light and dark contrast on Duchamp's neutral object. The dramatic lighting that casts a shadow across the top of the fixture gives *Fountain* its mysterious Buddha- or Madonna-like ap-

Steven Baldi
*Branded Light (Leica-Nikon)*, 2016
Detail of pl. 22

pearance. He selected as a backdrop the decorative pattern of a Marsden Hartley's painting (paintings appear as backdrops in other Stieglitz pictures such as his 1915 portrait of Francis Picabia; this compositional element brings the background even with the picture plane, thereby creating a shallow pictorial field in keeping with modern painting). As a proponent of straight photography, Stieglitz adhered to the rule that a true photograph was captured solely through the camera's lens rather than manipulated in the dark room. In essence, photographs document readymade subjects of the artist's choosing.

As the original *Fountain* disappeared soon after Stieglitz photographed it, this work is only known through this image in countless reproductions (mostly dating post-1959). Reproductions both devalue a work of art as it lacks the unique aesthetic experience of the original, and contribute to the aura of the work by making it widely accessible, thereby increasing its fame and desirability.[6] *Fountain*'s disappearance means there is no original; just the Stieglitz photograph and Duchamp's replicas and editions based on it. The photograph of *Fountain* by Stieglitz whets the appetite to experience the original, which is impossible as it no longer exists. Numerous contemporary artists have attempted to tackle this conundrum in their work. Richard Pettibone, known for appropriating photographs of famous icons of modern art in the scale of their reproduction, produced a series of miniature paintings of the Stieglitz photograph. Duchamp's work was central to Pettibone beginning in 1965. He used Stieglitz's photograph as a readymade image in several series of works, including *The Blind Man* series, 2015 (pl. 4; he also painted from photographs of the 1964 edition of *Fountain*). His practice was shaped by Duchamp's dictum that art is the process of choosing. As Pettibone notes, Duchamp was not saying "Just pick up anything," rather, he was proposing that artists should "pick and choose."[7] The work is the result of all the purposeful choices the artist makes. Pettibone chose to make paintings of photographs rather than re-photograph Stieglitz's image. Viewers are accustomed to perceiving the relation of scale in a photograph to the original subject; despite the small scale of an image, viewers assume the subject is life-size. Pettibone complicates this reading of photographs as his paintings are the *actual* size of their subject, that is, the photographic reproduction. His reliance on his sight rather than the mechanics of the camera to capture the image led to other paradoxes. Stieglitz's camera's depth of field and focus, and the studio lighting, distorted the image and obscured details. At the time he painted these works, Pettibone was losing sight in one of his eyes, which impaired his ability to see details in the shadows and blur of Stieglitz's photograph. As a result the works appear more painterly than photographic. Mimicking the serial nature of photographic reproduction, Pettibone installs his paintings in groupings of multiple canvases in the series. By setting up a comparison between each painting in a set, the slight variations become evident, and the work appears more human than that of its photomechanical source. Pettibone subtitled the series *Self-Portrait*, connecting his loss of sight to the title of the periodical that first published Stieglitz's photograph; after years of appropriating Duchamp's work, he had become "The Blind Man."

The cult of the original masterpiece was turned inside out by Sherrie Levine who since the 1980s has been appropriating the work of famous artists such as Man Ray, Piet Mondrian, and Duchamp. Her acts of appropriation comment on the recycling of art and ideas through history and face the anxiety of influence head on. As original works of art are known primarily through reproduction, Levine ponders how the reproduction shapes the viewer's perception. For *Fountain* (*Buddha*), 1996, Levine appropriated the Stieglitz photograph to create a sculpture (pl. 5). Much as Pettibone's works are paintings of the Stieglitz photograph, Levine's *Fountain* is a sculpture of the image of the urinal as depicted in the same photograph. Stieglitz's picture, while documenting the lost original, shrouds it in mystery as there are some details that are nearly impossible to decipher. As the photograph only shows *Fountain* from one angle, the other views are lost forever. The editions Duchamp made of *Fountain* in 1964 were based on blueprints from the Stieglitz photograph, which modified the distortions of the urinal caused by the foreshortened view that gave the fixture its squat Buddha-like shape. The 1964 editions, therefore, closely approximate the original urinal's proportions. Levine modeled her sculpture after the distorted image of the urinal in Stieglitz's photograph, producing a more compact form that matches the formal elegance and Buddha profile. By casting the work in bronze, the artist suggests that *Fountain* has achieved the lofty status as a masterpiece in the pantheon of art history. The material gives it a permanency that Duchamp's *Fountain* lacked, while the gesture of casting a work that is seminal to Levine's practice is akin to bronzing a baby's shoe.

Mike Bidlo, another appropriation artist, based his sculpture *Fractured Fountain* (*Not Duchamp Fountain 1917*), 2015, on the story recorded by Ira Glackens that his father, William Glackens, president of the Society of Independent Artists, smashed the urinal in order to resolve the controversy (pl. 6).[8] In his work, Bidlo imagined the smashed urinal mended and cast in the permanent medium of bronze, like Levine's *Fountain* (*Buddha*). Los Angeles artist Rachel Lachowicz picked up on another early rumor regarding Duchamp's *Fountain*; that he submitted it to the SIA on behalf of a woman friend. *Untitled* (*Lipstick Urinals*), 1992, composed of plaster and fiberglass urinals covered with cherry-red lipstick, is Lachowicz's feminist commentary on the male-dominated art world (pl. 7). Her arrangement of the urinals in a row on a wall restores the fixtures to their function so that the installation looks like a men's bathroom, a place where women are explicitly excluded. Lachowicz wryly combines references to men and women in this work, and brings to mind Duchamp's own attempt to disguise his gender with the invention of his female alter ego Rose (Rrose) Selavy in 1920.

The Stieglitz photograph of *Fountain* was published along with two articles defending the work in *The Blind Man*. One of these articles, "The Richard Mutt Case," praised the work for its transformative contribution to art. The anonymous author noted: "Whether Mr. Mutt with his own hands made the fountain or not has no importance. He CHOSE IT. He took an ordinary article of life, placed it so that its useful significance disappeared under the new title and point of view—created a new thought for the object."[9] Joseph Kosuth, one of the first Conceptual artists, extended this aspect of Duchamp's readymade to what he considered its inevitable conclusion in the mid-1960s. As long as the art work existed as a physical object it was subject to being evaluated according to the cultural codes of aesthetic opinions just like any other object in the world. For Kosuth, the "value" of particular artists could be "weighed according to how much they questioned the nature of art."[10] Without a physical form, art was exclusively linguistic in character. As Kosuth reasoned, art in its purest state is an "inquiry into the foundations of 'art,' as they come to mean."[11] His own work, as in his orange neon sign, *An Object Self-Defined*, 1966, is a language-based manifestation of the thought that formed it (pl. 8).

Although Kosuth proposed that the reduction of art to its essence as an idea was the only means to escape formalistic critiques, other artists saw the potential for inventing ways to produce physical art works that created new thoughts about the nature of art. The aesthetic decisions these artists made and the questions their works raised continued to give credence to the effectiveness of Duchamp's essential trinity of the aesthetic experience: artist, art work, viewer recognition. When Warhol made his Brillo boxes in 1964, it might have seemed as a repetition of Duchamp's gesture of creating a readymade out of a mass-produced, store-bought item (pl. 9). However, the distinctive characteristics of his Brillo box emerge by reviewing a litany of decisions Warhol made in its creation:

1. Warhol could have taken a store-bought Brillo box, but instead had his own boxes constructed out of wood on which he silkscreened the Brillo box design (he did not even use cardboard for the construction, because wood was a better surface on which to print).

2. Although he could have controlled the printing process to ensure that each print was uniform, he allowed the ink to drip and splatter and retained other imperfections. As a result of this process, each box is unique and attests to the human touch (even if it was not his hand), unlike the machine-made store-bought boxes.

3. Where Duchamp claimed he was indifferent to the formal properties of the items he chose for his readymades, Warhol selected a commercial design that adapted the tasteful graphics of modern

art—minimal abstract forms, with uninflected bold primary colors that reinforced the flatness of the surface. The Brillo box design, in fact, represented the epitome of modern taste, and yet, the idea of elevating such a mundane object to the heights of fine art was anathema to the criteria of modern art critics, who abhorred the contamination of kitsch.[12]

The Brillo box had one more thing going for it—it was "New!," which was a virtue in post-World War II consumer culture, as well as the avant-garde. The graphics on Warhol's box announced it was "New" and improved over the art of the past. The reaction to the Brillo boxes when Warhol first exhibited them at the Stable Gallery, in 1964, echoed the initial response to Duchamp's *Fountain*. Some were jolted by what Duchamp called the aesthetic echo of the work, others found pleasure in knowing that it was considered a significant work of art, while the rest dismissed it as a joke or a bad work of art.[13] Warhol made other works based on boxes for Campbell's Tomato Juice (pl. 10) and Del Monte Peach Halves, but the Brillo box so succinctly embodied the new thought for this object that it overshadows the others.

Jeff Koons also picked up on the issues that *Fountain* raised with his vacuum cleaner works of the late 1970s and early 1980s that launched his career. His series *New Hoover Convertibles* consisted of the newest models of vacuum cleaners, which Koons selected and enshrined within fluorescent illuminated Plexiglas vitrines so that they would retain their newness or virginity. Like Duchamp's urinal and Warhol's Brillo box, the vacuum cleaners also signaled cleanliness and hygiene—clearly a virtue and a desirable state in twentieth-century America. The vacuum cleaners like the Brillo box also celebrate the tastefulness of modern industrial design. The Hoover company employed market research to produce vacuums that would appeal to consumers' taste and stoke desire—color, style, attachments, etc. Desire was built into the vacuum cleaner's design and was ready made for Koons' use. Desire is also built into Koons' works that use children's toys as a subject. Inspired by his own happy childhood memories, Koons chose to model his first sculptures in the late 1970s after cute inflatable flowers and toys made out of the same vinyl material as the originals, as well as subsequent works such as the balloon dog sculptures made of porcelain or highly polished stainless steel (pls. 11, 12). Brightly colored, friendly, and erotically suggestive, these sculptures seem to pose no threat to viewers except as a challenge to their definition of art.

Duchamp's readymades, as well as Warhol's and Koons' works, were removed from their everyday use and elevated as art by being displayed in places where one would expect to see art—galleries, museums, collections, art publications, etc. Los Angeles artist Jorge Pardo tested other facets of the issues *Fountain* raised. Pardo belongs to the first generation of visual artists to use computers as a tool for creating art and to communicate through the Internet.[14] This early exposure to computer technology radicalized his thoughts about categorization and socialization. Like Duchamp, Pardo designated mundane objects as art. For his career-defining 1990 exhibition at Thomas Solomon's Garage in West Hollywood (a former garage), Pardo filled the gallery with objects one would expect to find in a suburban garage. The space appeared to be part workshop and part storage area, housing tools and supplies such as a router table, wrenches, a plank of wood, a ladder, etc. (pl. 13). Although most of the everyday objects in the exhibition were pre-existing, Pardo altered them so as to render them useless as tools or domestic items. In almost every case, he substituted the common, utilitarian material of the original object with rare and exotic woods that could be admired for their material beauty but rendered the item impractical for use. Unlike Duchamp, who submitted *Fountain* into an art exhibition with the expectation that it would be shown as an art work within the gallery context, Pardo reverted Solomon's gallery back to its original function as a garage by installing objects that one might expect to find in a typical household garage. These objects were not displayed on pedestals or framed on the wall. Rather they were scattered around the space just like their utilitarian counterparts would be distributed. This arrangement provided Pardo the opportunity to investigate what constitutes an aesthetic experience. In particular, he speculated on what separates an art experience from an everyday experience, especially when his work looks like furniture in a domestic setting (pls. 14, 15). If the art work looks like everything else in the room and exists in the same space as everyday objects, how does one know he or she is having an aesthetic experience?

Pardo belongs to a loosely identified group of artists that includes Felix Gonzalez-Torres, Philippe Parreno, Rirkrit Tiravanija, among others, who practice "relational aesthetics," a term coined by French critic Nicolas Bourriaud in the mid-1990s.[15] These artists expanded the viewer's role in the essential relationship Duchamp established between artist, art work, and viewer. Rather than treat the art work as a self-contained, autonomous object, they created social situations in which the art work is always changing in relation to the context it is displayed and to the viewer's response.

Much as the computer influenced Pardo's conception of categorization and the socialization of the aesthetic experience, digital technology shaped Cory Arcangel's relocation of the aesthetic experience within the virtual world of the web. One of his best-known early gestures consisted of modifying cartridges for video games such as Super Mario Brothers and reintroducing his version, *Super Mario Clouds*, 2002, onto the web where categories are fluid. Arcangel's version could be found through a variety of searches; users could search for Super Mario Brothers video game, or seek out art works by Arcangel. Both searches would lead to the same site where Arcangel's work could be accessed. The experience was shaped by the search engine rather than the art context. His creation could be both art and not art.

In the video *Apple GarageBand Auto Tune Demonstration*, 2007, Arcangel appropriated footage of Jimi Hendrix's famous "Star Spangled Banner" performance at the fabled Woodstock rock concert in 1969, and ran it through Apple's digital audio workstation GarageBand Auto Tune, which makes music production widely accessible (pl. 16). The strident chords that made Hendrix's ballad a unique and original piece of artistry are automatically corrected by the Apple program so that it conforms to ideal norms of pitch. Initially, this work seems to be critiquing the homogenization of art through technology, until one realizes that Arcangel has, in fact, created an original work of art in the process that heightens the audience's sensitivity to how technology has vastly altered the aesthetic experience.

Arcangel also explored the aesthetics of the web in his redesign of websites. Graphics and fonts are the virtual face of a brand, company, institution, or individual. For his own website, he chose a utilitarian, un-artsy style that fit the do-it-yourself hacker manual approach of his work (www.coryarcangel.com).

The access to a wide range of images in cyberspace and the web's collapse of traditional categories and context for art works shape the perception of artists and viewers alike. Elad Lassry uses found generic photographs sourced from print magazines, advertising, Hollywood headshots, and the Internet, along with photographs he shoots in the studio (pls. 17–20). He exhibits these images in brightly colored frames that match the dominant hues of the photograph and gives them a three-dimensional presence.[16] The overall aesthetic is derived from commercial photography of the 1970s and 1980s rather than the tradition of fine art photography. The significance of Lassry's enterprise becomes evident when these works are viewed in groups rather than individually. Although they look like slick commercial photographs, details such as double-exposures and overlays of silkscreened dots alert viewers to reconsider their initial assumption about the classification of these objects as art. Conversely, Steven Baldi creates collages of various camera brands—Leica, Zeiss, Canon, etc.—that he dramatically illuminates in his studio and photographs through Plexiglas to produce distorted and refracted effects (pls. 21–24). These works appropriate the process of Stieglitz's straight photography in that the camera, rather than Photoshop techniques or dark room manipulation, produced the elegant black-and-white prints that embody the medium's modern aesthetics.

Duchamp's *Fountain* was more than a commentary on authorship and originality. He used this work to make a distinction between the aesthetics of a work from that of style and taste. For Duchamp, taste was acquired and a condition of a culture, whereas aesthetics was self-contained in the work itself and could be experienced only by the rare viewer who had the innate ability to be receptive to its emotional jolt. His friend and frequent collaborator Francis Picabia similarly grappled with these issues in his late "kitsch" paintings of the 1930s and 1940s. Like Duchamp, he frequently switched styles and art genres, thereby avoiding the production of a signature look. The two exhibited at the Armory Show in New York, 1913, with Picabia showing his radical abstract paintings. Both were active in the post-World War I Dada art movement in New York and Paris, and Duchamp's *L.H.O.O.Q.*, 1919, was initially known from the version Picabia created for reproduction in his periodical *391*, March 1920. (In Picabia's version of Duchamp's "rectified readymade," Leonardo da Vinci's *Mona Lisa* is sporting a mustache, but is missing the goatee that Duchamp included in his original work.) While Duchamp abandoned painting, Picabia continued to explore its potential. A skilled draftsman and an adept copyist, he shocked many of his admirers with his crude late paintings, and they were even excluded in his retrospective in the Guggenheim Museum in New York, 1970[17] (pls. 25, 26). Some even accused Picabia of aiming to appeal to the taste of Nazi officers. It is plausible, however, that Picabia used these paintings as an exegesis on taste and aesthetics, much as Duchamp had previously explored with *Fountain*. Most of these late paintings were painted during the Nazi period, while Picabia was living in France. Picabia's Dada work along with all forms of abstraction and modern art was declared "degenerate" by the Third Reich. The 1937 Degenerate Art Exhibition, assembled by the Reich Propaganda Directorate, Culture Office, aimed to "appeal to the sound judgment of the people and thus to put an end" to degenerate modern art. The Nazi regime empowered the "forward-looking" German people as "the natural standard-bearers of an art of the Third Reich."[18] In late 1941, Picabia wrote to Gertrude Stein: "[My painting] has become more and more the image of my life and of life in general, but of a life that neither can nor wishes to contemplate the world in all its greed and monstrousness."[19] He further lamented that "Everything that was moral in art is dead. Fortunately. It is the only benefit we have received from the cataclysm that surrounds us."[20] Art drained of morality was beyond judgments of good and bad. As an artist so deeply invested in the avant-garde, it is possible to imagine Picabia pondering why his abstract and Dada works were labeled degenerate while the Nazis sanctioned a derivative classicism that bordered on kitsch. His paintings provided the means to puzzle out this conundrum. Duchamp stated that he chose his readymades out of ambivalence to their formal qualities, but Picabia seems to have selected his sources specifically because they were bad and ran contrary to his own taste and the standards of the avant-garde. While critics scorned Picabia's late paintings during his lifetime, these works attracted new appreciation over the last twenty-or-so years as his influence on artists widened. Duchamp was a great admirer of his friend's work and in 1925 purchased paintings directly from him, representing his various approaches, which he sold the following year for a significant profit. A statement made by Duchamp in 1949 suggests he comprehended the motivation behind Picabia's late paintings as a response to fascist ideology, noting that Picabia "could be called the greatest exponent of freedom in art, not only against academic slavery, but also against slavery to any given dogma."[21]

Julian Schnabel is among the artists who emerged in the 1970s who were influenced by Duchamp's and Picabia's explorations regarding aesthetics, taste and style. He, like Picabia, deliberately selected a source outside the canon of fine art as his subject in his series, *Veramente Bestia*, 1988, which is comprised of paintings he scavenged in thrift stores. Virtually all of Schnabel's paintings are created with the same process; painted and various other methods of mark-making applied onto a found or constructed surface. The painting's support creates a tension between the categories of figuration and abstraction—when Schnabel uses a distressed or weathered material such as tarpaulins or awnings as the support for his paintings, they look like abstract paintings, whereas figurative backgrounds cancel out the abstract dabs and swooshes he applies on the surface. Even when he brushes a line right across the eyes of a thrift store portrait of a young girl in *Veramente Bestia V (Girl with No Eyes)*, 1988 (pl. 27), the work is still perceived as figurative rather than abstract. These found backgrounds also influence the viewer's value judgment. *Girl with No Eyes*, painted on an amateur thrift store painting, consequently may be considered a bad painting, whereas Schnabel's series of paintings on stunning Kabuki theater backdrops, 1989, are heralded for their beauty, even though both types of works are comprised of similar painted gestures.

For his neon sign, *Ordinance No. C-14-23*, 2014, Miami artist Tom Scicluna combines the medium of Kosuth's ponderous conceptual work with an appropriation of the word "aesthetics" by the City of Fort Lauderdale for its ordinance on homelessness to justify the city's banning of human waste and the storage of personal possessions on public property (pl. 28).[22] Created for an exhibition at NSU Art Museum concerning homelessness, this work relocates the "interest in aesthetics" to its rightful place in an art museum.

Duchamp's early experiences with juried art exhibitions made him suspicious of the process. In 1912, his *Nude Descending a Staircase, No. 2*, 1912, was rejected by the Salon des Indépendants in Paris. Even though the American Society of Independent Artists exhibition in 1917 advertised that it would display the work of any artist who paid the entry fee, his *Fountain* was rejected on grounds of immorality. Throughout his career he questioned who had the right to judge art works. His views were published in a statement in the catalog of the Bel Ami International Art Competition and Exhibition, 1946–47: "Jurors are always apt to be wrong. The only argument in favor of this jury is that the three differed in their selection of the first, second and third prizes, showing how close the decision was. But even the conviction of having been fair does not change my doubts on the right to judge at all."[23] This statement was appropriated by the Paris-based artist collective that goes by the name of Claire Fontaine (pl. 29), a fictional artist like R. Mutt. (The name itself is a readymade drawn from the popular brand of French notebooks, Clairefontaine. The name also puns on the title of Duchamp's *Fountain*.) The artists used the statement as a readymade subject for their illuminated sign with the text appearing as it did in the printed catalog. With no attempt to apply standards of graphic design, it has the indifference to style and taste of a Duchamp readymade, and it boldly challenges the viewer to offer a judgment on its artistic merits. Claire Fontaine also took the step to manufacture an aura for this work by placing it on a light box. The effect of the light box is not reproducible in a catalog or book, and therefore, the work itself maintains the ability to startle the viewer with its power and beauty. Like illuminated advertisements, this work stands out in exhibitions and lures the viewer with its light.

The deliberation on the aesthetic value of a work was a subject taken up by several contemporary artists. The influential Los Angeles Conceptual artist John Baldessari wryly addressed this issue in his series of photographs *Choosing: Green Beans*, 1972 (pl. 30). In each photograph a finger points to one of three beans. Each new trio exhibits a variety of different sizes and shape. The viewer, however, is kept in the dark as to the criteria for the selection. Moreover, it is also difficult to decipher the rules from visual evidence alone as there is no consistency in the shape or size of bean chosen. Originally an Expressionist painter, Baldessari recalls thinking: "If they [Duchamp and Warhol] are right, then I'm wrong."[24] *Choosing: Green Beans* mirrors the turmoil in the art world in the 1970s when the pluralism of art production made the traditional formal analysis of art obsolete, and new criteria had yet to be established.

Among the works in the exhibition, are photographs by Los Angeles artist Judy Fiskin from her series *Some Aesthetic Decisions*, 1990, that aestheticize objects, architecture and interiors that do not conform to conventional taste (pls. 31–35). She continued to explore this subject in other series including *Some Art* (pls. 36–39). Fiskin diverges from Duchamp's distinction between taste and aesthetics as she perceives both to be a condition of specific cultures. In a 1988 interview she noted: "For every era of art-making there is some new agreed-upon code."[25] Like Baldessari with his *Choosing: Green Beans*, Fiskin explored how looking at art is an "activity that depends on consensus." She observed that "if the consensus dies, then the object is up for redefinition."[26] Her photographs transform these observations into a "visual experience" that leaves the viewer feeling unmoored. Her early photographs of flower arrangements particularly succeed in exposing the construct of taste and judgment. She was drawn to the competitive world of flower arranging displays at the time, as she wanted to study a world traditionally dominated by middle-class and upper-middle-class women for whom flower composition was their only creative outlet. There were strict rules and guidelines for these arrangements that were used by the judges of these competitions. What appeared tasteful within this milieu ran counter to Fiskin's own sensibility as a Conceptual artist. In her photographs of these arrangements, she mediated the viewer's response to her subjects by overlaying them with her own process, which, in turn, ran contrary to the norms of fine art photography; the prints are each approximately only 1 ¾ x 2 ¾ inches or 2 ½ inches square, the edge of the negative is maintained rather than cropped, and the white integral frames transform the photograph into a sculpture.[27] Fiskin shifted her focus from the objects that were under consideration for judgment to the act of choosing in her video *50 Ways to Set the Table*, 2003, in which she documented the jury deliberation of a table-setting competition (pl. 40). Despite the good intentions of the jury to adhere to set criteria and to remain objective, personal taste and politics compromised the results.

Although Fiskin aimed to expose the arbitrary nature of aesthetic decisions, the series reveals the potential for creative expression even within the strict guidelines of flower arranging and table-settings. The serial nature of the work of German photographers Bernd and Hilla Becher likewise reveals the potential for aesthetic choices within the same typological structures, such as water towers and grain elevators (pl. 41). The couple began photographing industrial structures around 1957, using the same straightforward, black-and-white format, and adjusting the scale so that size between types of structures was uniform. The framed photographs were grouped in a grid, which allowed for comparisons of the wide range of styles and architectural solution for each type of structure. If form follows function, the architects and/or engineers found room for embellishment that varies considerably from one site to another.

To create her series, *The Blind*, 1986, French artist Sophie Calle interviewed individuals blinded from birth who provided her with descriptions of beauty (pls. 42–44). Her project consists of combining the photographic portraits of the individuals she interviewed, text excerpted from their remarks, and a photograph of an object, person or scene that each described as beautiful. Although Calle never revealed her intentions for this project, it provides an opportunity for viewers to ponder whether beauty is solely the construct of the sighted. One participant concludes that the color green is beautiful, "because every time I like something I'm told it's green. Grass is green, trees, leaves, nature too," while another finds hair "magnificent," especially African hair. He submits to this beauty, noting: "I curl up in women's long hair. I pretend I'm a cat and meow." Yet another man reported that he had been told that the sea was beautiful: "They tell me it is blue and green and that when the sun reflects in it, it hurts your eyes. It must be very painful to look at." Touch and intimate relationships are among the unifying characteristics of these descriptions of beauty. Detached from the sense of sight, beauty for these individuals is emotional and personal.

Duchamp shifted the role of judge from the jury or art professional to each individual viewer, acknowledging that only a few would have the ability to truly respond to the inherent aesthetics of a work of art. What happens if there is no criteria for judging and there are no official arbiters of art such as museum curators and critics? What if art is judged on the consensus of popular taste? The dissident Russian collaborative art team Komar and Melamid (disbanded since 2003–04) did just that by enlisting poll services in several countries to widely survey the public about the characteristics that would make the "most wanted" painting and the "most unwanted" painting in their *People's Choice* series, 1994–97 (pl. 45). They relinquished their privileged position as artists to make aesthetic decisions to the majority, and produced "the most wanted" and "least wanted" for each country based on the poll results. The prints they produced in their *People's Choice* portfolio, 1995, include the charts and statics from these surveys.

In today's age everyone gets to judge art by expressing likes or dislikes on Facebook or posting images on Pinterest and Instagram among other sites and applications. As critic Rob Colvin recently noted, this on-line culture has hastened the advent of a whole genre of "Like Art," that is "art that looks very much like art you've already seen, that you know very well, and that you already like . . . it's 'the look for less,' with no greater aesthetic aspirations. It lives for heart taps, thumbs-up clicks, and space on people's walls—digital or brick-and-mortar."[28] These examples might seem like the juryless utopia Duchamp proposed. However, the result is the opposite of Duchamp's goal as they tend to perpetuate the familiar rather than plucking out works that resonate with the true aesthetic echo.

In the 1970s, feminist theory challenged the hierarchy of art, toppling painting from its pinnacle. Painting, with its long trail of male artists, was challenged by the devalued field of crafts, which was especially associated with women's work. Los Angeles artist Mike Kelley contributed a new thought to art in the late 1980s with his works made from handcrafted toys and quilts that he found in thrift stores (pl. 46). The decade of the 1980s witnessed the unbridled commodification of art, especially for new work by young artists. Kelley aimed to create work that escaped its escalation to a commodity. The objects he chose to use were labor-intensive crafts created for children or loved ones. As these works were gifts, there was no monetary exchange. Nevertheless, Kelley recognized that there was a "price" associated with these items, but it was "repressed" as they embodied the love of their creator, typically a close relative or friend.[29] As Kelley observed, "the gift operates within an economy of guilt, an endless feeling of indebtedness attends it because of its mysterious worth."[30] The recipient remains forever in the debt of the creator, as its value in the "love-hours" it took to create these objects could never be repaid. The results of all this labor are objects made of cheap or lowly materials that have no intrinsic value, except to the creator and the recipient. The saddest cut of all is that they ended up as cast-aways in thrift stores. Kelley chose these found objects much as Duchamp selected the urinal for *Fountain*, with the distinction that the original urinal was a commodity with an assigned monetary value even before Duchamp acquired it, but that its value as an art work was elevated once Duchamp transformed it into a work of art. The handcrafted items Kelley selected were low in the hierarchy of artistic expression, yet they were loaded with an emotional weight that was priceless. As Kelley noted, the fine art "junk sculpture" (the assemblages of found objects in the spirit of Duchamp) "could be said to have value *in spite* of its material value, while the craft item could be said . . . to have value *beyond* its material."[31] Duchamp's readymades acquired their aura through the artist's act of transformation, whereas Kelley employed the readymade aura of his materials for his work. Despite Kelley's goal to create works that functioned outside of the realm of the monetary system, his art works quickly became commodities in the art market, where value was assigned.

African American artist Kara Walker used crafts associated with the antediluvian American South (traditionally created by amateurs, particularly women), such as cut-paper silhouettes, for her seminal works of the 1990s (pls. 47, 48). For most of the twentieth century, the art world tended to value African tribal art and black outsider art and crafts as more racially authentic than art by African American artists working in modern and contemporary art modes, such as abstraction.[32] Walker's silhouettes emit conflicting messages that scramble their meaning and significance: this is work created by an African American Conceptual artist that elevates craft to high art, and recasts derogatory stereotypes of African Americans in new configurations of racial and gender power structures.

As early as 1949, Duchamp bemoaned the role the art market played as the arbiter of a work's significance. He noted: "The great public, today, is guilty of having introduced as a criterion the quantative evaluation of the work of art, the market value: people today often buy paintings as an investment."[33] By the end of the twentieth century, artists such as Richard Phillips recognized that there was no escaping the commodification of art. Phillips turned to making exquisitely executed paintings of some of the most highly valued art works in today's market, such as Jeff Koons' garish porcelain sculpture of pop star Michael Jackson and Gerhard Richter's highly desirable abstract paintings (pls. 49–51). Like Kelley's thrift store assemblages, Phillips' readymade subjects have a built-in aura as rare commodities, weighted with monetary value and the heft of art history. He dares the viewer to appreciate his paintings without thinking of the precious subjects or styles he has copied. As market value and art historical opinion fluctuate with time, what happens to this aura if the works Phillips appropriated become worthless? Phillips gets the last laugh as his works demonstrate how the age-old tradition of painting can actively perpetuate the legacy of Duchamp's readymade, *Fountain*.

The discourse on aesthetics, taste, and value judgments that *Fountain* ignited in 1917, was rooted primarily in Western art history and art practice and caught up in the contemporary consumer economy. It was created at a specific juncture in art history when painting was speeding towards abstraction. Duchamp's readymades were no longer representations of reality, they were real objects. Duchamp considered them a rupture in the trajectory of art since Impressionist painting, which, in his opinion, primarily appealed to the sense of sight rather than the intellect.[34] *Fountain* was introduced in New York at a time when many of its artists were pursuing a distinctly American modernism that was not derivative of French art.[35]

While *Fountain* created a new thought about art, it is important to recognize that it is not the only way to think about art, especially from the perspective of non-Western cultures or art that preceded the Renaissance. In the twelfth century, for instance, Abbot Suger of France proposed a concept of art in the service of God that launched the Gothic style, in which the material splendor of the golden doors of the Basilica of Saint-Denis in Paris and its lofty stain glass windows would elevate the mind to the spiritual and the "True Light."[36] For the young, contemporary Malawi-born artist Samson Kambalu, the importance of gift-giving in his village provided an alternative paradigm for judging a work's success. Predominantly an agricultural society, the economy of the East-African nation of Malawi was based on gift-giving rather than a monetary system. After crops were planted the villagers had considerable time on their hands as they awaited the harvest. The greatest gift one could bestow on fellow villagers was to provide them with opportunities to waste time through play. Kambalu conceived his short films as gifts that would waste the viewer's time. If the viewer finds pleasure in his work, it is good (pl. 52). One hundred years after Duchamp submitted *Fountain* to the Society of Independent Artists exhibition, this transformative action continues to reverberate as a catalyst in overcoming the conventions of taste. Most of all it opens up the possibilities for artists to consider a multitude of aesthetic decisions that may lead to new thoughts concerning the nature of art.

[1] William A. Camfield, *Marcel Duchamp Fountain* (Houston: Houston Fine Art Press, 1989), p. 19.

[2] Francis M. Naumann and Hector Obalk, eds., *Affectionately, Marcel: The Selected Correspondence of Marcel Duchamp* (Ghent and Amsterdam: Ludion), 2000, p. 47.

[3] Marcel Duchamp, "Apropos of 'Ready-mades'," talk delivered at the Museum of Modern Art, New York, October 19, 1961, in Michel Sanouillet and Elmer Peterson, eds., *The Writings of Marcel Duchamp* (New York: Da Capo, 1989), p. 136. Reprint, originally published: *Salt Seller* (New York: Oxford University Press, 1973).

[4] Anonymous author, "The Richard Mutt Case," *The Blind Man*, no. 2 (May 1917).

[5] Among the other milestones that ignited interest in Duchamp in the late 1950s and early 1960s were the publication of Robert Lebel's monograph in 1959, which revealed the full scope of his production to a new, receptive audience, and the presentation of his first retrospective at the Pasadena Art Museum, Pasadena, CA, curated by Walter Hopps. The opening was attended by Andy Warhol, in town for his exhibition of Campbell's Soup Can paintings at Los Angeles' Ferus Gallery, Los Angeles artists Edward Ruscha, Larry Bell, Billy Al Bengston, Ed Moses, Edward Kienholz, and Robert Irwin, and actor Dennis Hopper. See Dickran Tashjian, "Nothing Left to Chance: Duchamp's First Retrospective," in Bonnie Clearwater, ed., *West Coast Duchamp* (Miami Beach: Grassfield Press, 1991), pp. 61–83.

[6] Walter Benjamin's essay on the subject of aura and reproduction (first published in German in 1935, first revised English edition, 1939) was especially influential, see Walter Benjamin, "The Work of Art in the Age of Mechanical Reproduction," in *Illuminations*, trans. Hannah Arendt (New York: Schocken Books, 1986), pp. 18–42.

[7] Richard Pettibone, *The Blind Man: A Conversation about Marcel Duchamp with Richard Pettibone and Kristy Caldwell* (New York: Castelli, 2016), p. 13.

[8] Ira Glackens, *William Glackens and the Eight: The Artists Who Freed American Art* (New York: Horizon Press, 1957), p. 188.

[9] Anonymous author, "The Richard Mutt Case."

[10] Joseph Kosuth, "Art After Philosophy, I and II," in Gregory Battcock, ed., *Idea Art: A Critical Anthology* (New York: E. P. Dutton, 1973), pp. 80–81. Reprinted from *Studio International* (October and November 1969).

[11] Kosuth, "Art After Philosophy, I and II," p. 93.

[12] The influential American art critic Clement Greenberg aimed to establish new criteria to evaluate modern art using a formal analysis. For Greenberg abstract painting made these formal qualities more apparent than figurative works, which he perceived as complicating the viewing process by diverting attention to the figurative subject matter. Paintings that successfully reduced painting to its fundamentals: pigment on the flat surface of the picture plane, i.e. the color field paintings of Morris Louis and Larry Poons were held in his highest regard. In Greenberg's breakout essay, "Avant-Garde and Kitsch," *Partisan Review* (Fall 1939), he stated: "The nonrepresentational or 'abstract,' if it is to have aesthetic validity, cannot be arbitrary and accidental, but must stem from obedience to some worthy constraint or original.... Picasso, Braque, Mondrian, Miró, Kandinsky, Brancusi, even Klee, Matisse and Cézanne derive their chief inspiration from the medium they work in. The excitement of their art seems to lie most of all in its pure preoccupation with the invention and arrangement of spaces, surfaces, shapes, colors, etc., to the exclusion of whatever is not necessarily implicated in these factors." Reprinted in Clement Greenberg, *Art and Culture: Critical Essays* (Boston: Beacon Press, 1961), pp. 6–7. At the time he wrote "Avant-Garde and Kitsch," Greenberg feared that the "ruling class," which was historically the source of support for the avant-garde, was being seduced away from "high art" by kitsch, "popular, commercial art and literature with their chromeotypes, magazine covers, illustrations, ads, slick and pulp fiction, comics, Tin Pan Alley music, tap dancing, Hollywood movies, etc., etc." (Greenberg, p. 9). To Greenberg, kitsch is "mechanical and operates by formulas," it is "vicarious experience and faked sensations" (Greenberg, p. 10). Warhol's work, as well as that of other Pop artists, met all the conditions of kitsch as defined by Greenberg, except that they stimulated the viewer's imagination and consciousness like Duchamp's *Fountain*.

[13] Philosopher Arthur Danto recorded his epiphany upon his first encounter with Warhol's *Brillo Box* at the Stable Gallery, New York, 1960, in Arthur C. Danto, *After the End of Art: Contemporary Art and the Pale of History* (New Jersey: Princeton University Press, 1997), pp. 123–24.

[14] Pardo's class at Art Center College of Design in Pasadena, CA, in the late 1980s, was also the first to be given Apple Computers, see Bonnie Clearwater, *Jorge Pardo: House* (North Miami: Museum of Contemporary Art, 2007), p. 8.

[15] Nicolas Bourriaud, *Relational Aesthetics*, trans. Simon Pleasance and Fronza Woods with the participation of Mathieu Copeland (Paris: Les Presses du réel, 2002); French edition, 1998.

[16] Elad Lassry interview by Christopher Bollen, *Interview Magazine*, November 25, 2008.

[17] *Francis Picabia*, Solomon R. Guggenheim Museum, New York, 1970.

[18] Stephanie Baron, *"Degenerate Art": The Fate of the Avant-Garde in Nazi Germany* (Los Angeles: Los Angeles County Museum of Art, 1991), pp. 360, 362.

[19] Annette Johansen and Margrit Brehm, eds., *Café Dolly: Picabia, Schnabel, Willumsen / Hybrid Painting* (Ostfildern: Hatje Cantz, 2013), p. 130.
[20] *Café Dolly: Picabia, Schnabel, Willumsen.*
[21] *Affectionately, Marcel*, p. 58.
[22] See Fort Lauderdale Ordinance: C-14-42. This work was created for the exhibition *Research and Development: Concerning Belonging*, NSU Art Museum Fort Lauderdale, June 1 to September 14, 2014.
[23] In 1964 Duchamp served as a juror for the Bel Ami International Art Competition and Exhibition of New Paintings by Eleven American and European Artists (circulated by the American Federation of Arts). The other judges were Alfred H. Barr, Jr. (first director of the Museum of Modern Art, New York) and New York art dealer Sidney Janis.
[24] *West Coast Duchamp*, p. 90.
[25] "Interview with Judy Fiskin," by John Divola, in Virginia Heckert, *Some Aesthetic Decisions: The Photographs of Judy Fiskin* (Los Angeles: J. Paul Getty Museum, 2011), p. 18.
[26] "Interview with Judy Fiskin."
[27] Virginia Heckert, "Judy Fiskin's Aesthetic Decisions," in Heckert, *Some Aesthetic Decisions: The Photographs of Judy Fiskin*, p. 2.
[28] Rob Colvin, "Everbody Likes 'Like Art,'" *Hyperallergic*, March 1, 2017.
[29] Mike Kelley in *Rubell Family Collection: Highlights and Artist's Writings*, vol. 1 (Miami: Rubell Family Collection / Contemporary Arts Foundation, 2014), p. 176.
[30] *Rubell Family Collection.*
[31] *Rubell Family Collection.*
[32] See Lowery Stokes Sims, "Artists, Folk and Trained: An African-American Perspective," in Thomas J. Lax, *When Stars Begin to Fall: Imagination and the American South* (New York: The Studio Museum of Harlem, 2014), pp. 22–31.
[33] *West Coast Duchamp*, "Appendix A," p. 114.
[34] *West Coast Duchamp*, "Appendix A," p. 108.
[35] See Sarah Greenough et al., *Modern Art and America: Alfred Stieglitz and His New York Galleries* (Washington, DC: National Gallery of Art and Boston, New York, London: Bulfinch Press, Little Brown and Company, 2000) for a discussion on early modernism in America. William Glackens, president of the Society of Independent Artists, also served as the chairman of the American committee for the Armory Show in 1913. As NSU Art Museum Senior Curator Barbara Buhler Lynes notes in the text for the museum's exhibition *William Glackens: A Modernist in the Making* (September 4, 2015 to December 2017), the Armory Show had been a disappointment to its American artists, particularly Glackens, because their work, in his mind, did not reveal a national American modernism. She further remarks how Glackens and Charles and Maurice Prendergast set out to explore solutions to this problem, including consulting sources on art from India and Ceylon.
[36] Abbot Suger of Saint-Denis recorded his accounts of the rebuilding and redecorating of the Abbey of Saint-Denis, Ile-de-France (dedicated 1140), in his *De Administratione*. He wrote about the role of art in the service of God as "transferring that which is material to that which is immaterial," see Whitney S. Stoddard, *Art and Architecture in Medieval France* (New York, Evanston, San Francisco, London: Icon Editions / Harper & Row, 1972), pp. 375–78.

# WORKS

1. Alfred Stieglitz
*Fountain*, 1917
Photograph of *Fountain*
by Marcel Duchamp
11 x 8 1⁄16 inches

Fountain by R. Mutt | Photograph by Alfred Stieglitz

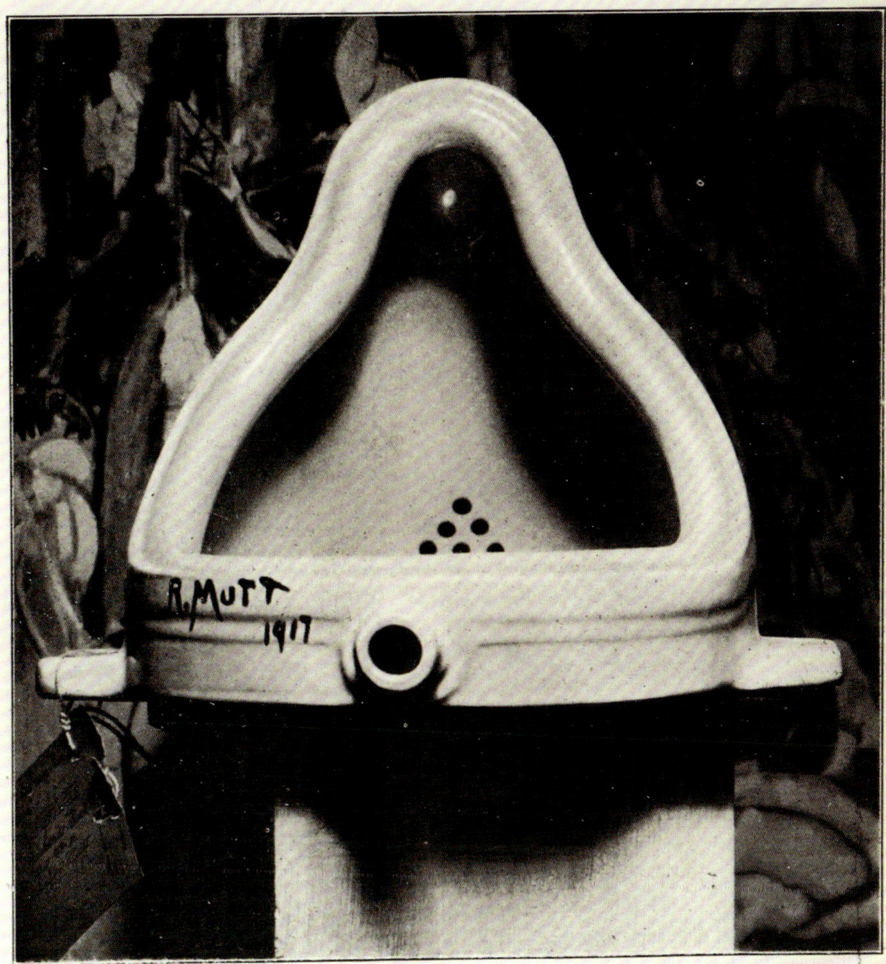


THE EXHIBIT REFUSED BY THE INDEPENDENTS

2. Marcel Duchamp
*Boîte-en-valise (De ou par Marcel Duchamp ou Rrose Sélavy) (The Box in a Valise [Of or by Marcel Duchamp or Rrose Sélavy])*, 1941/1961
Mixed media, edition 1 of 30
16 x 15 x 4 inches

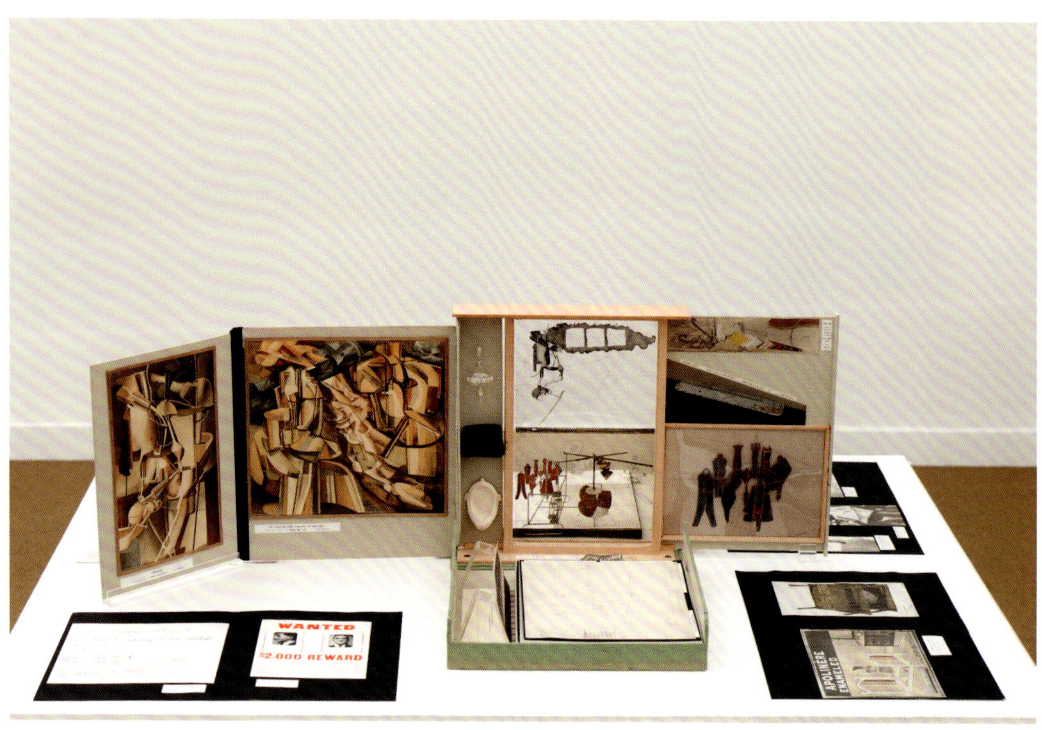

3. Marcel Duchamp
*Trébuchet (Trap)*, 1917, 1964
Wood and metal, edition of 7
7 3/8 x 39 3/8 x 4 7/8 inches

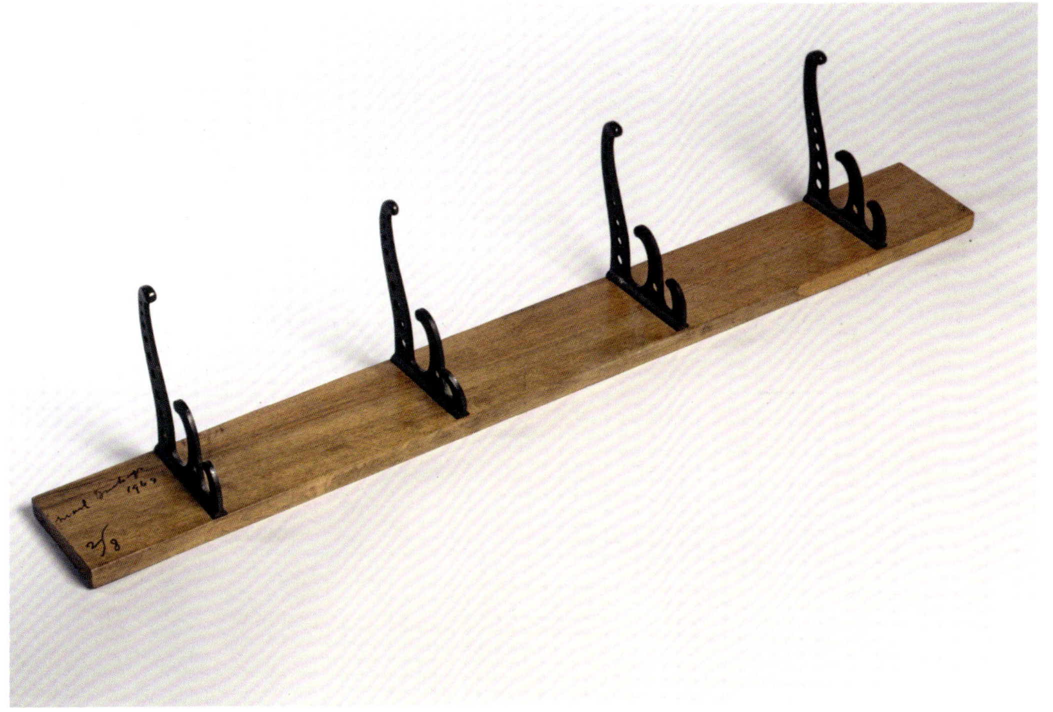

4. Richard Pettibone
*The Blind Man*, 2015
Oil on canvas (6)
5 7/8 x 5 inches
7 1/2 x 6 1/4 inches
8 3/4 x 7 1/2 inches
10 1/4 x 8 3/4 inches
11 5/8 x 10 inches
14 1/4 x 11 3/4 inches

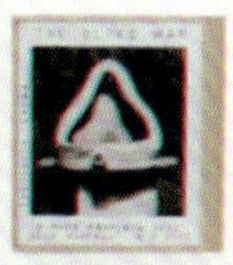
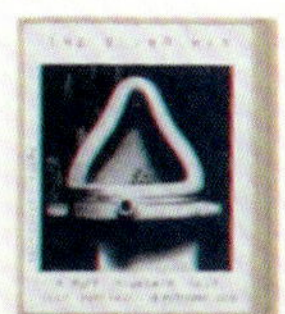
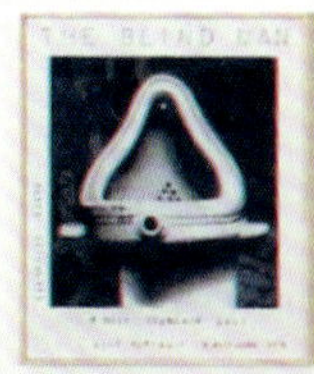

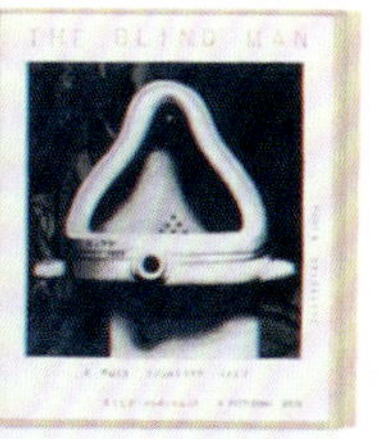
THE BLIND MAN

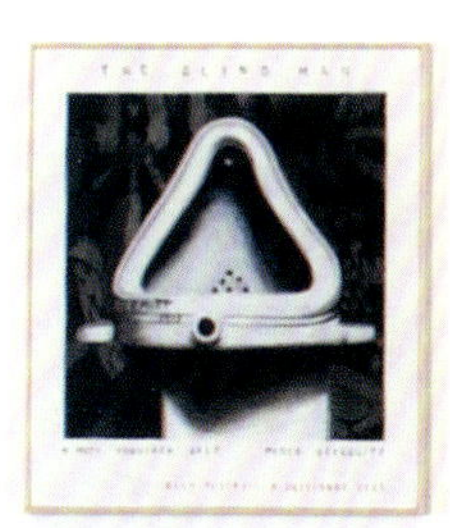

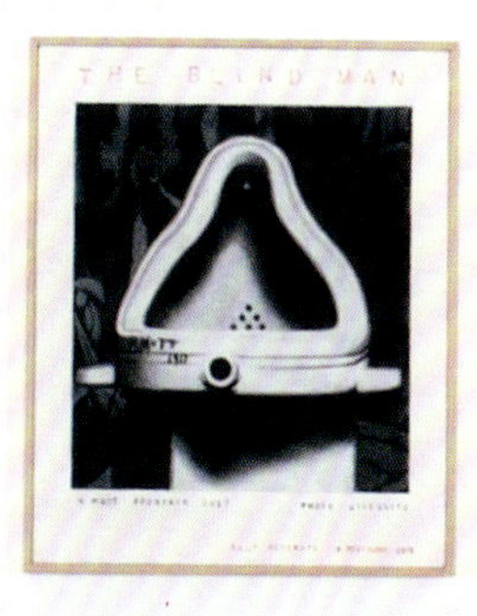
THE BLIND MAN

5. Sherrie Levine
*Fountain (Buddha)*, 1996
Bronze
12 x 17 x 16 inches

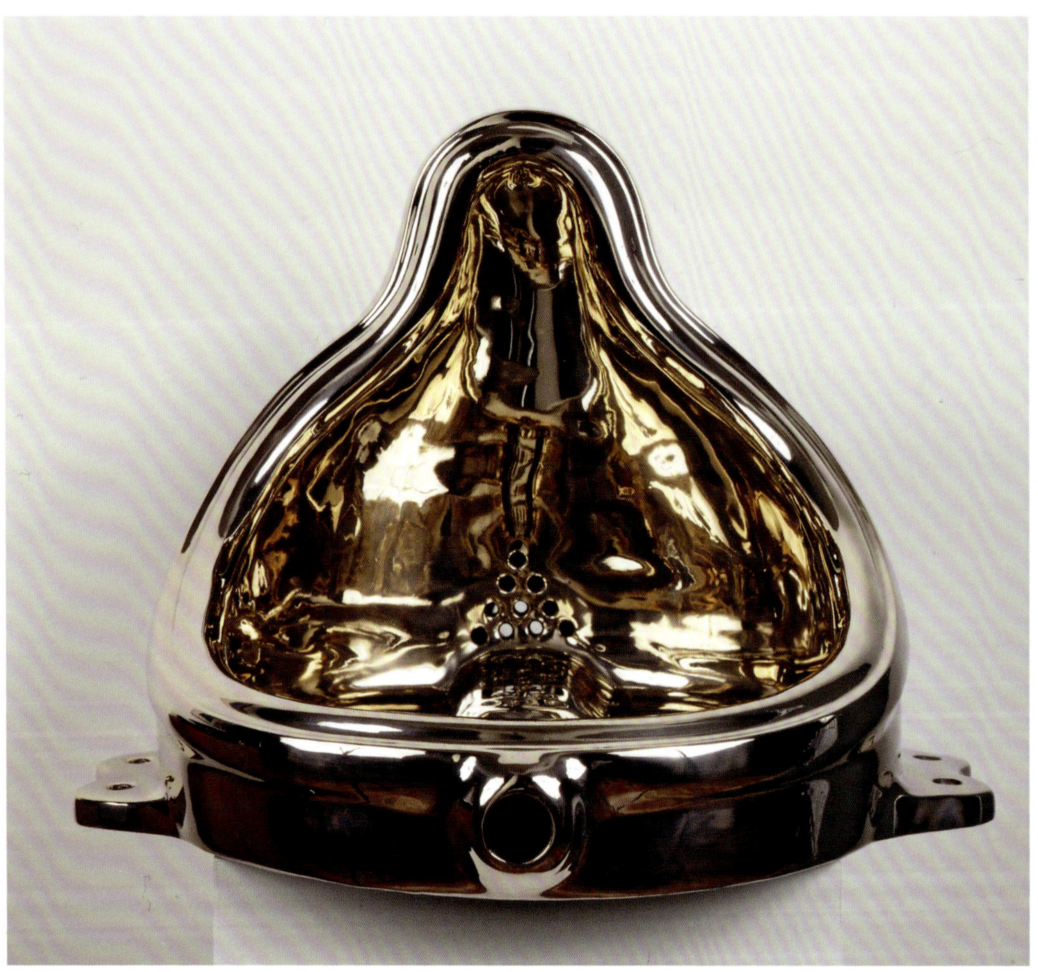

6. Mike Bidlo
*Fractured Fountain*
*(Not Duchamp Fountain 1917)*,
2015
Bronze, edition of 8
14 3/4 x 16 x 11 inches

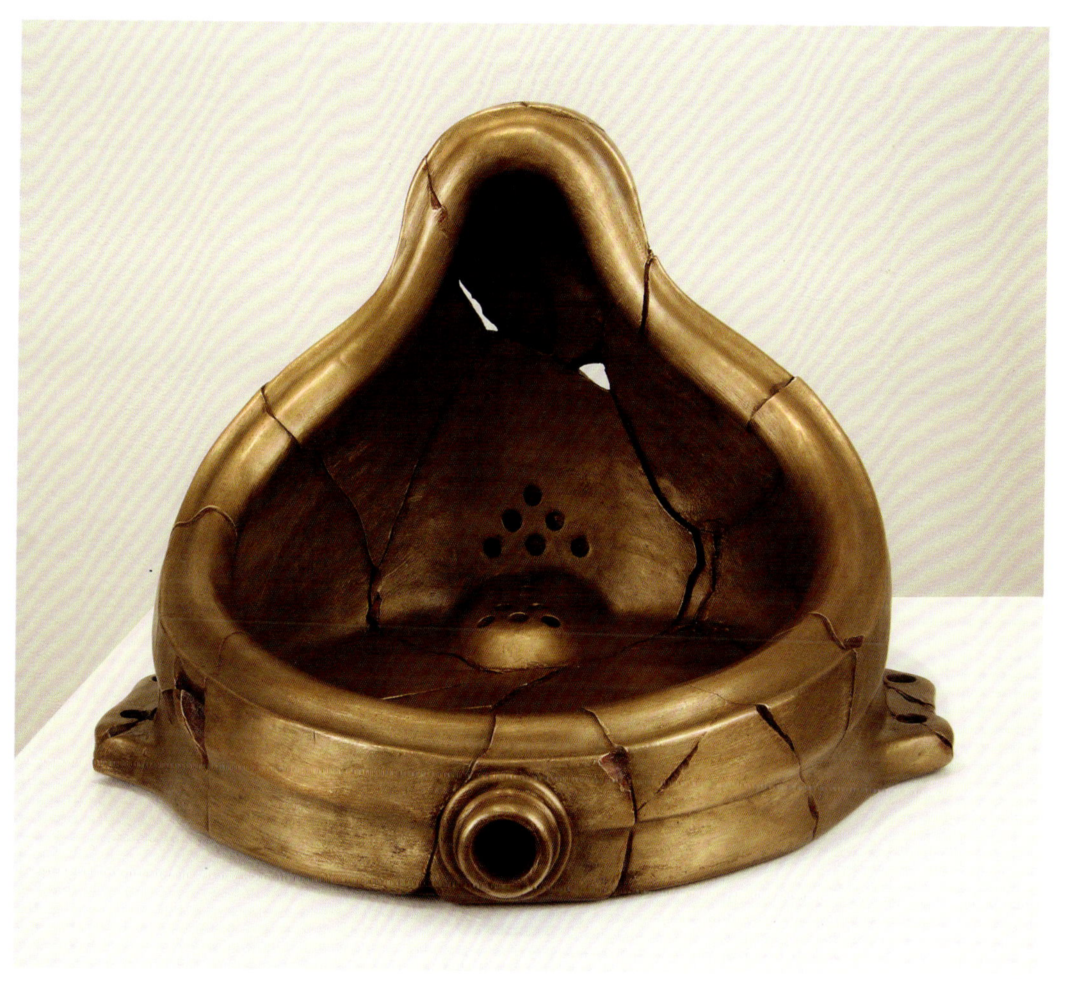

7. Rachel Lachowicz
*Untitled (Lipstick Urinals)*,
1992
Lipstick, wax, plaster,
fiberglass
15 x 9 x 6 inches

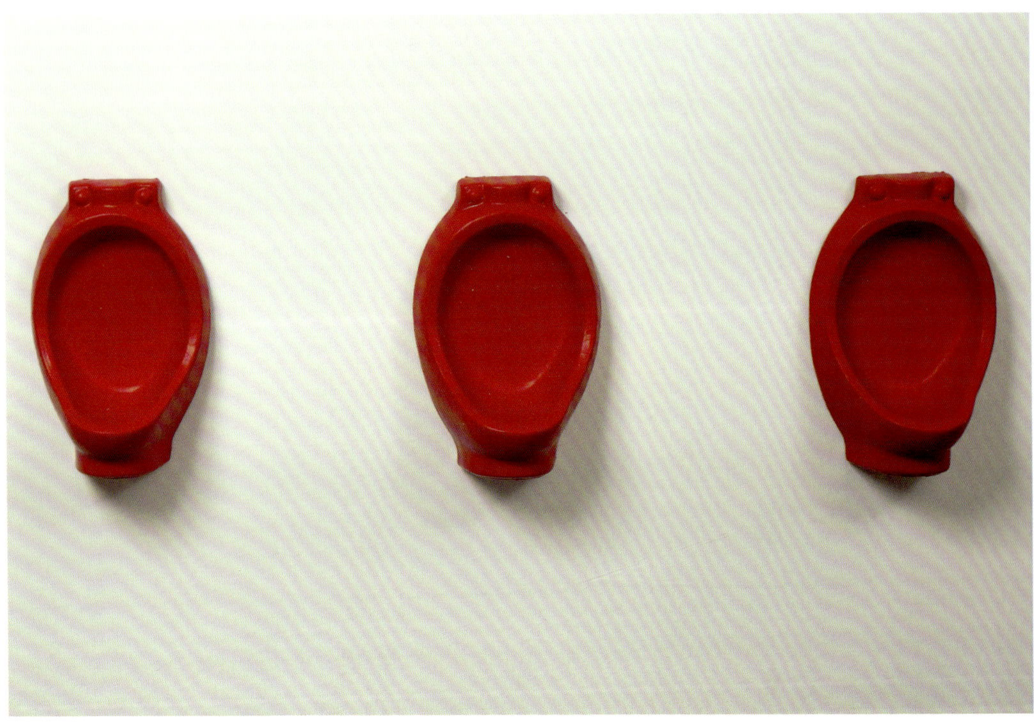

8. Joseph Kosuth
*An Object Self-Defined*, 1966
Orange neon mounted on wall
4 x 68 inches

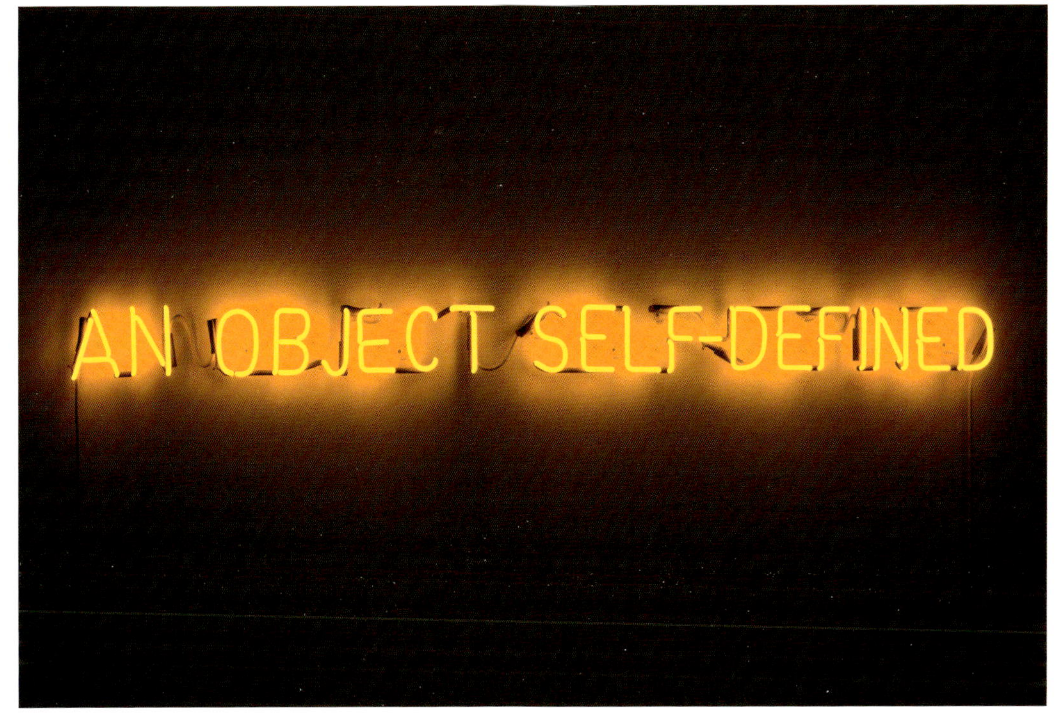

9. Andy Warhol
*Brillo Soap Pads Box*, 1964
Silkscreen ink and house paint on plywood
17 x 17 x 14 inches

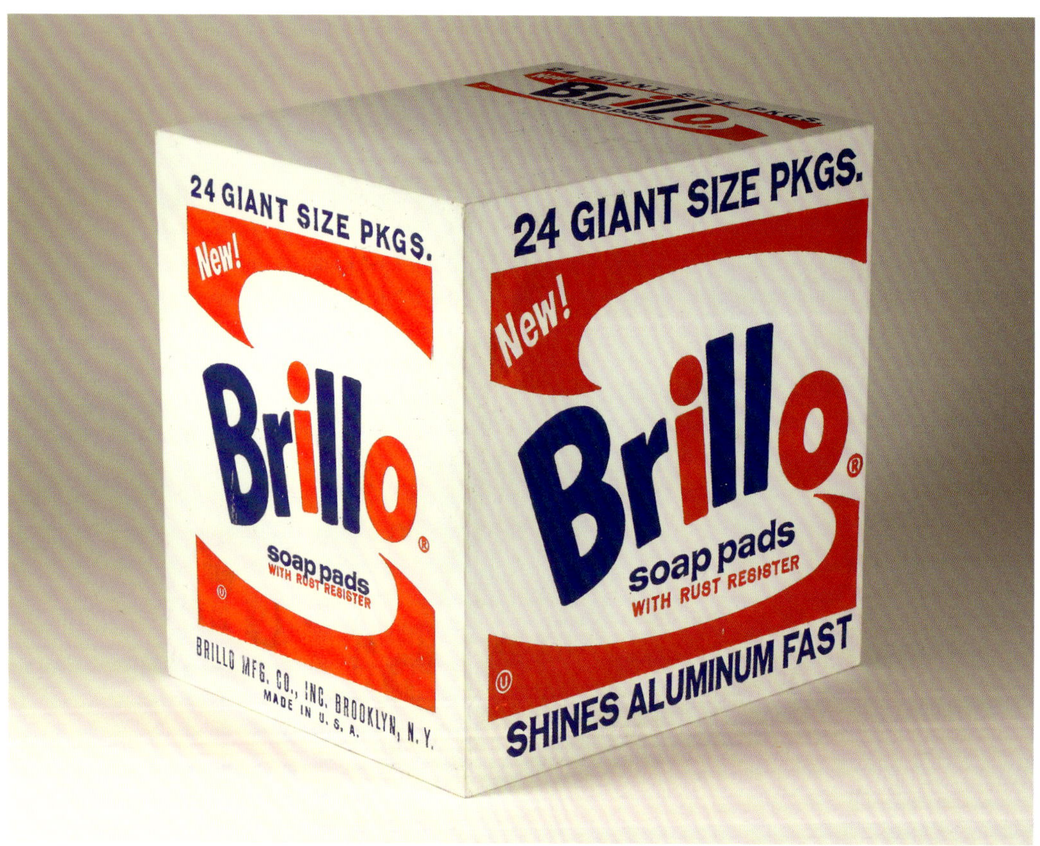

10. Andy Warhol
*Campbell's Tomato Juice Box*,
1964
Silkscreen ink and house
paint on plywood
10 x 19 x 9 ½ inches

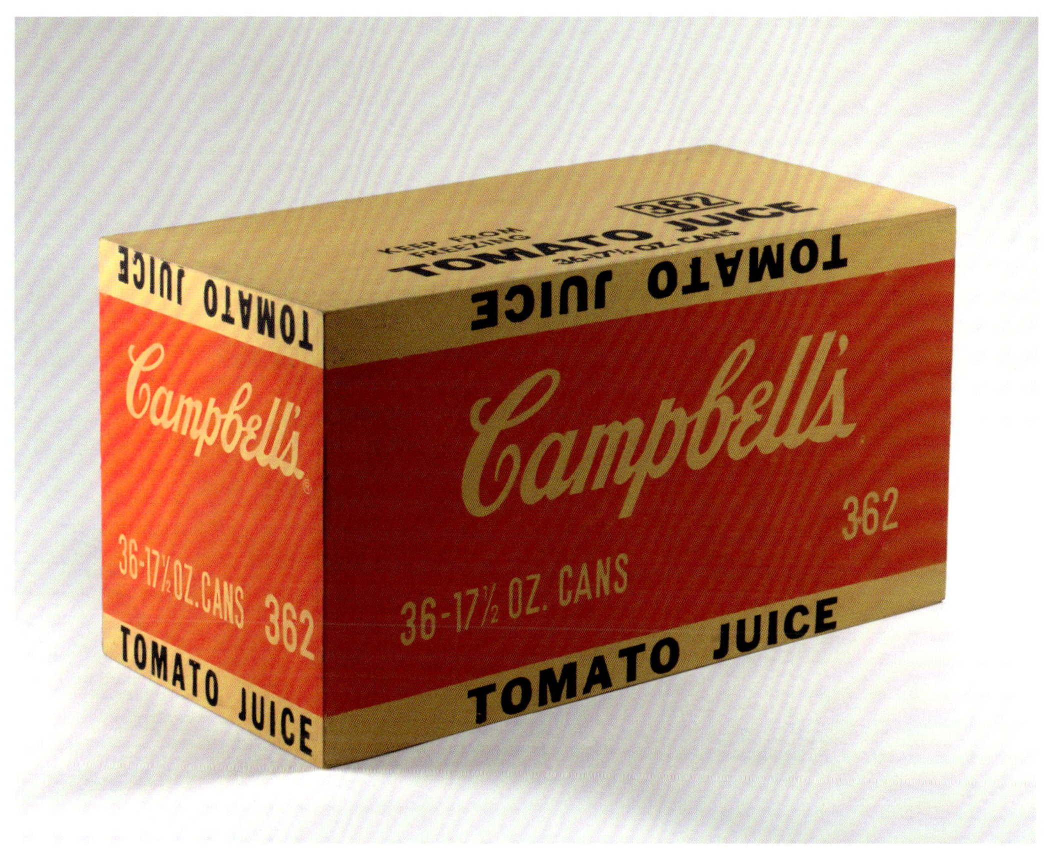

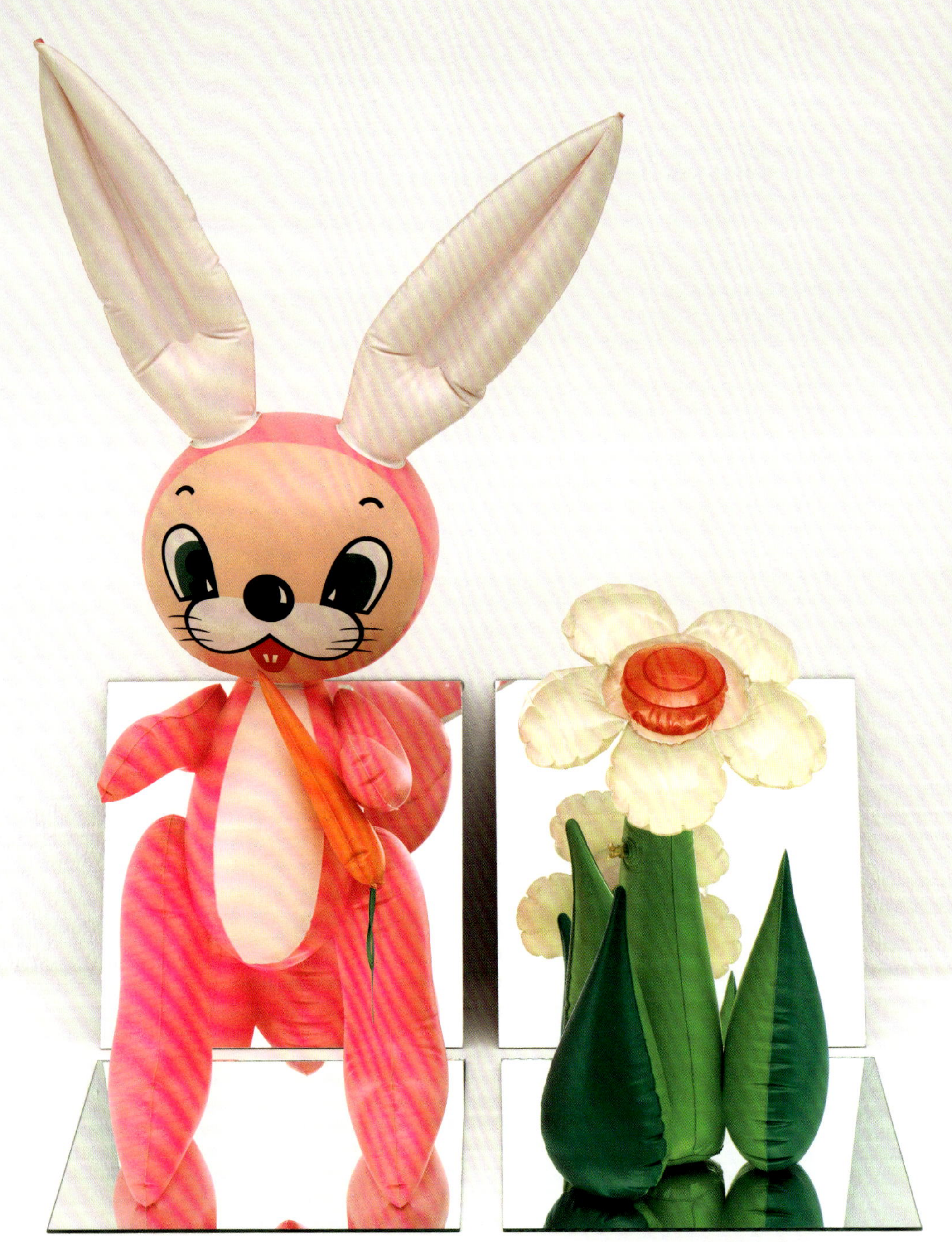

11. Jeff Koons
*Inflatable Flower and Bunny (Tall White, Pink Bunny)*, 1979
Vinyl, mirrors
32 x 25 x 19 inches

12. Jeff Koons
*Balloon Dog (Blue)*, 2002
Porcelain, edition of 2300 plus 50 APs
10 ½ x 10 ½ x 5 inches

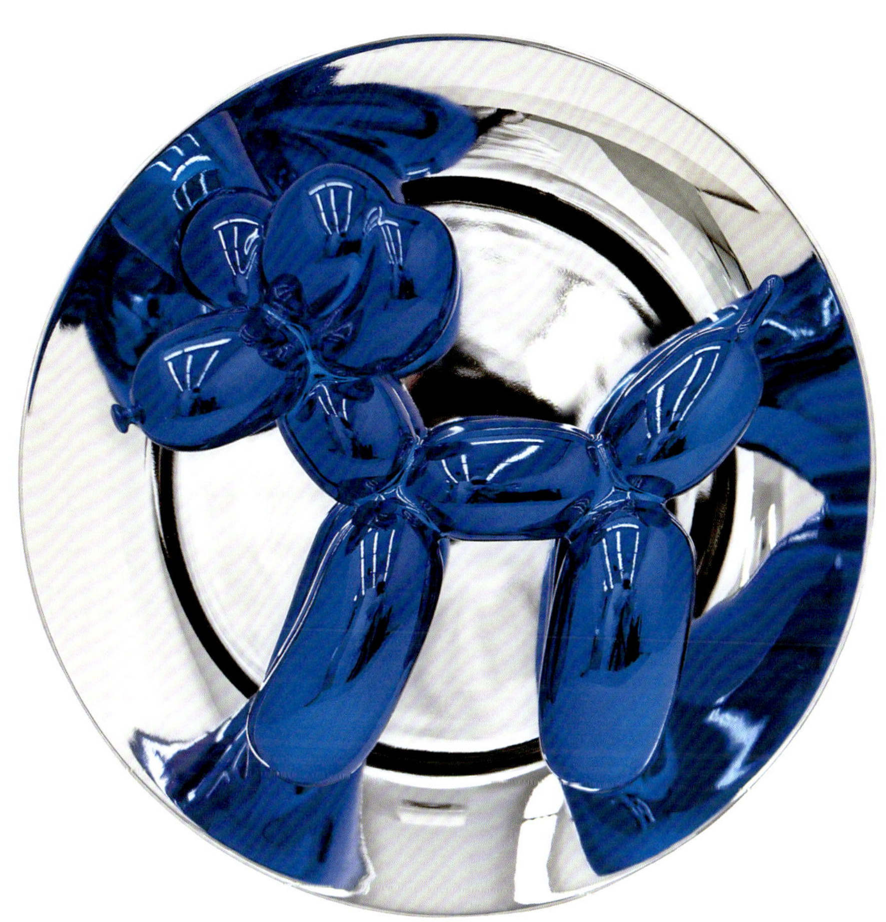

13. Jorge Pardo
*Palette*, 1990
Oak wood, 16 penny nails,
Danish oil
40 x 27 ¼ x 5 inches

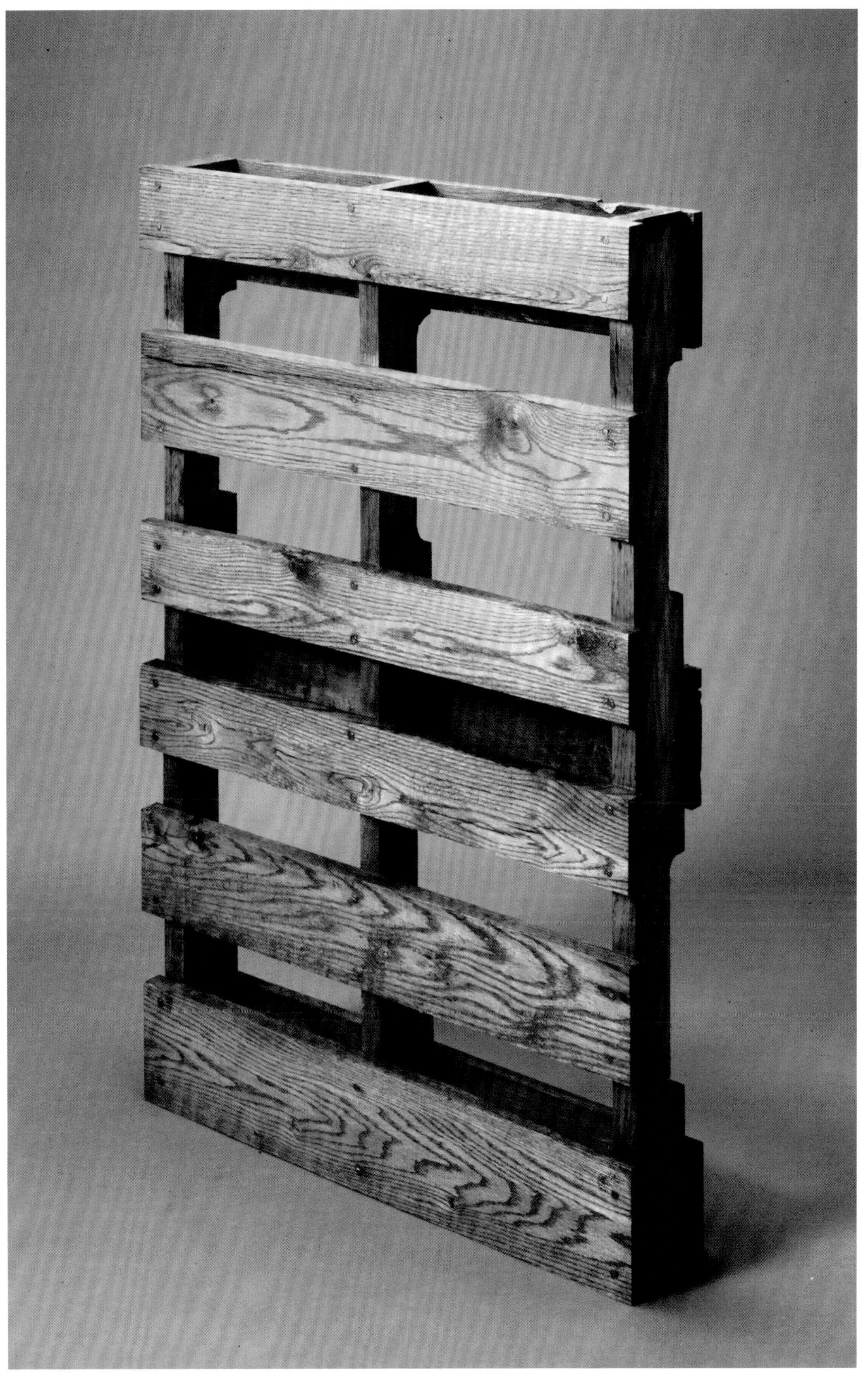

14. Jorge Pardo
*Le Corbusier Chair*, 1990
Welded copper pipes
26 x 30 x 33 ¼ inches

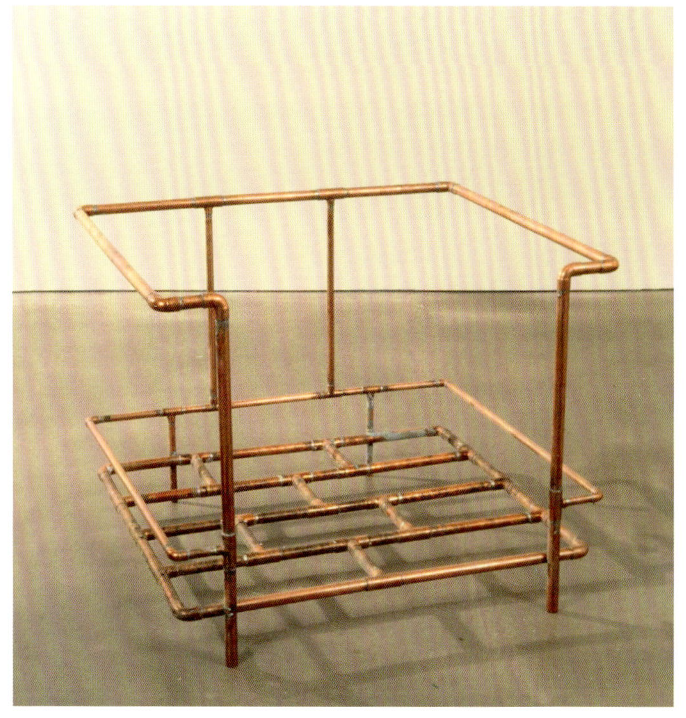

15. Jorge Pardo
*Le Corbusier Sofa*, 1990
Welded copper pipes
26 x 64 x 30 inches

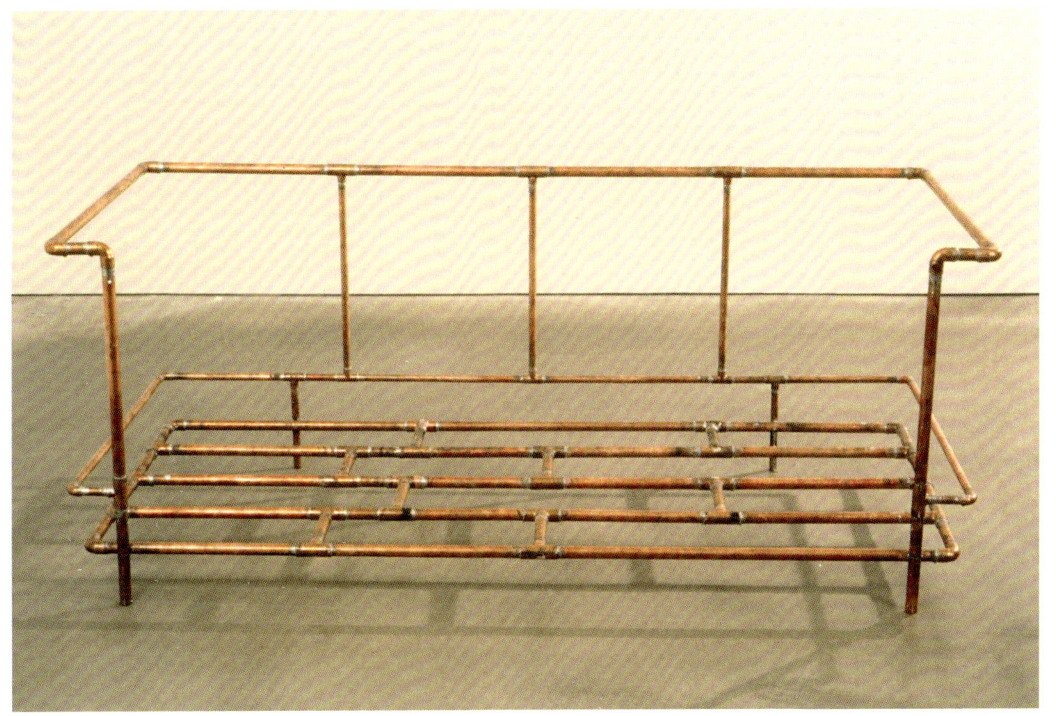

16. Cory Arcangel
*Apple GarageBand Auto Tune Demonstration*, 2007
Film projection from a digital source
8 minutes, 48 seconds

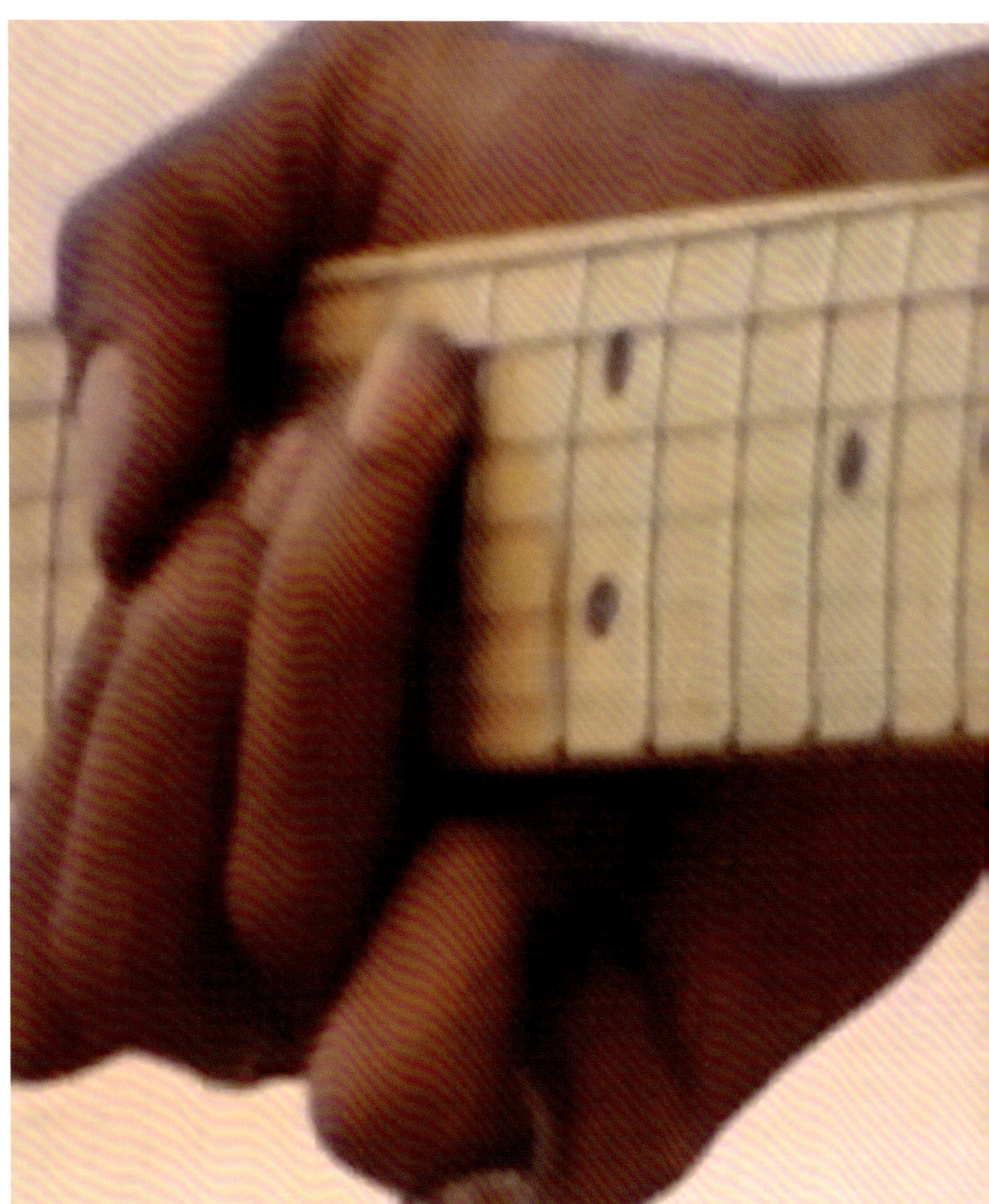

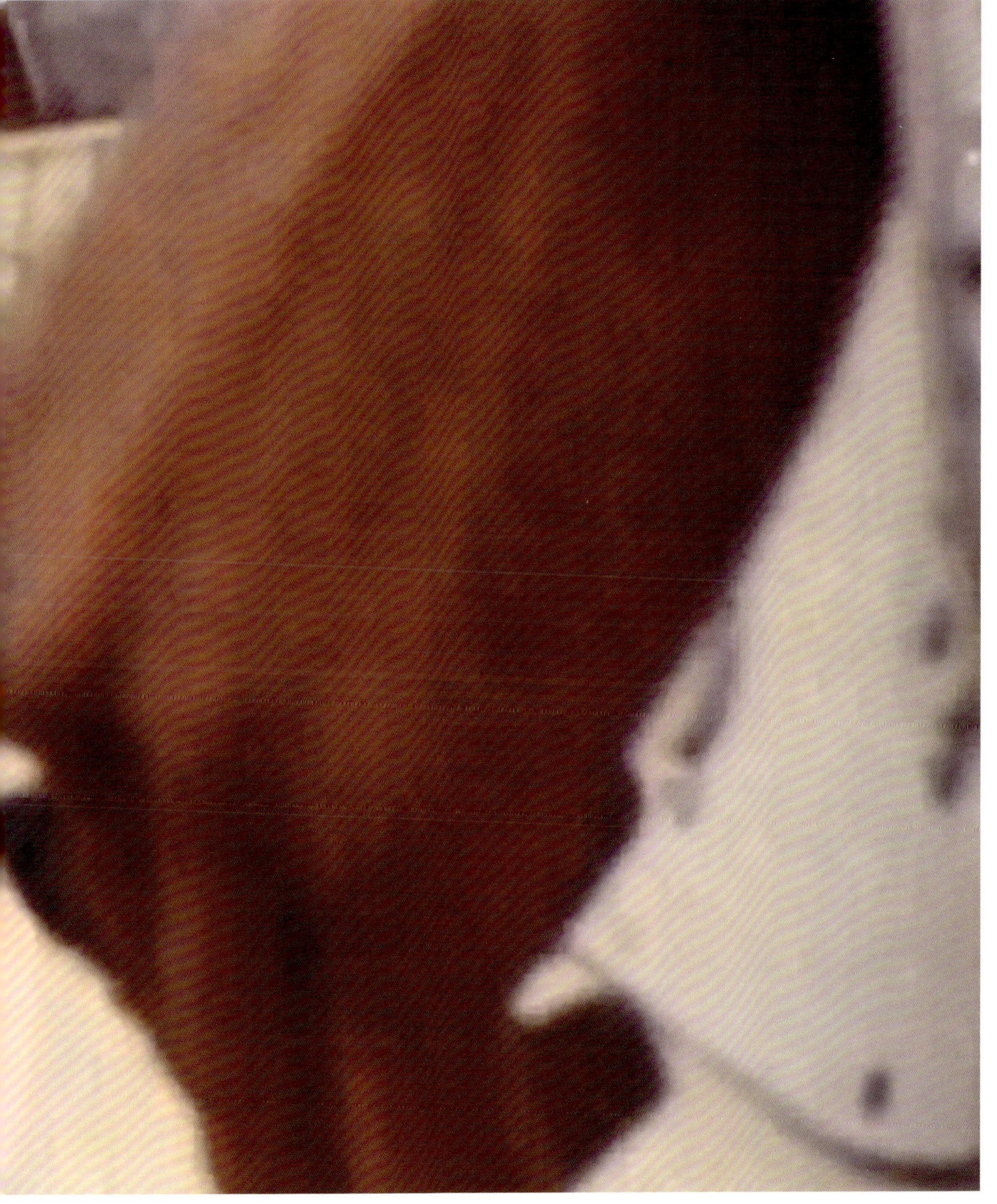

17. Elad Lassry
*Man*, 2007
C-print, edition 5 of 5
plus 2 APs
14 x 11 inches

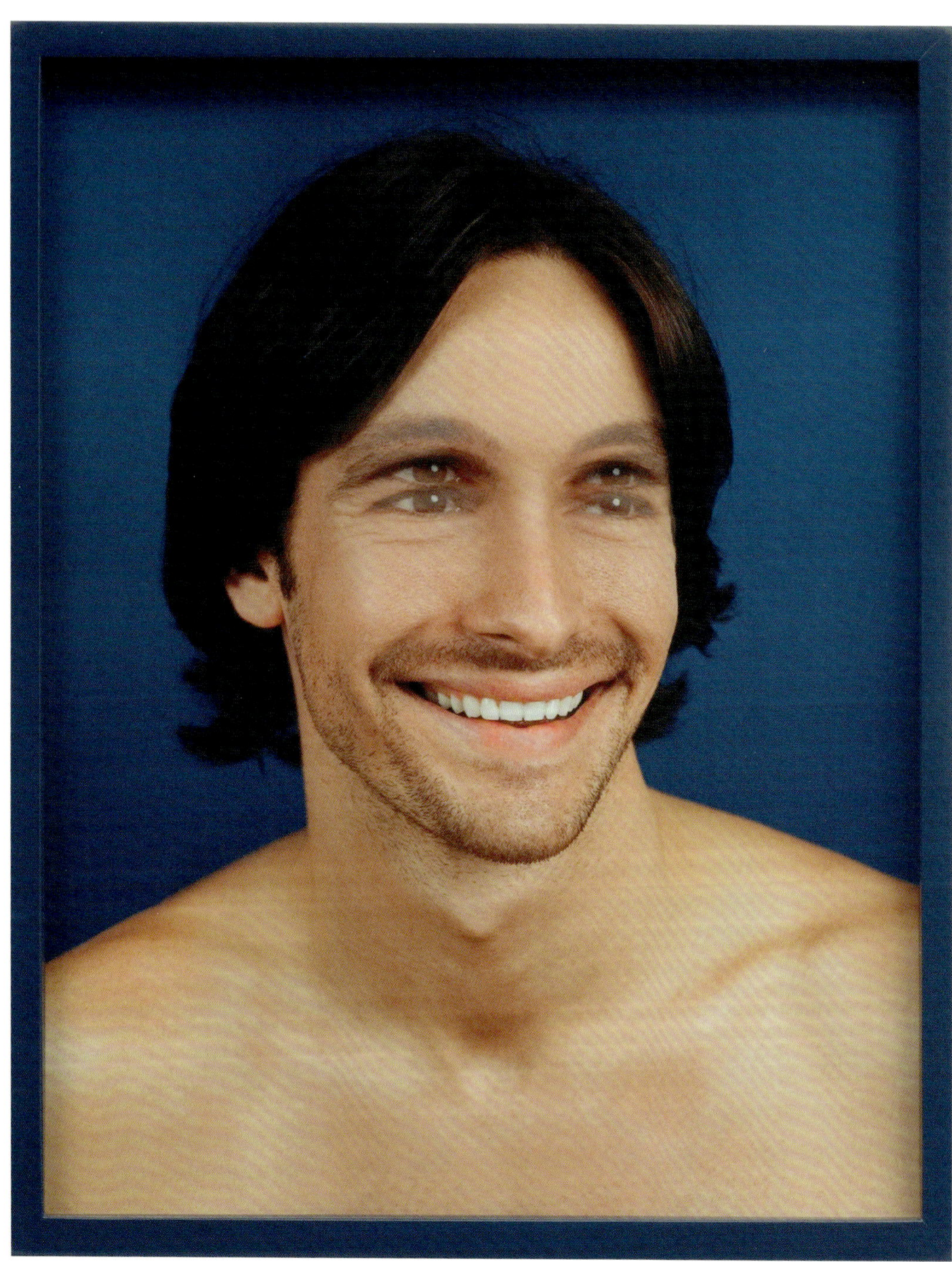

18. Elad Lassry
*Czech Girl*, 2009
C-print, edition 3 of 5
plus 2 APs
14 x 11 inches

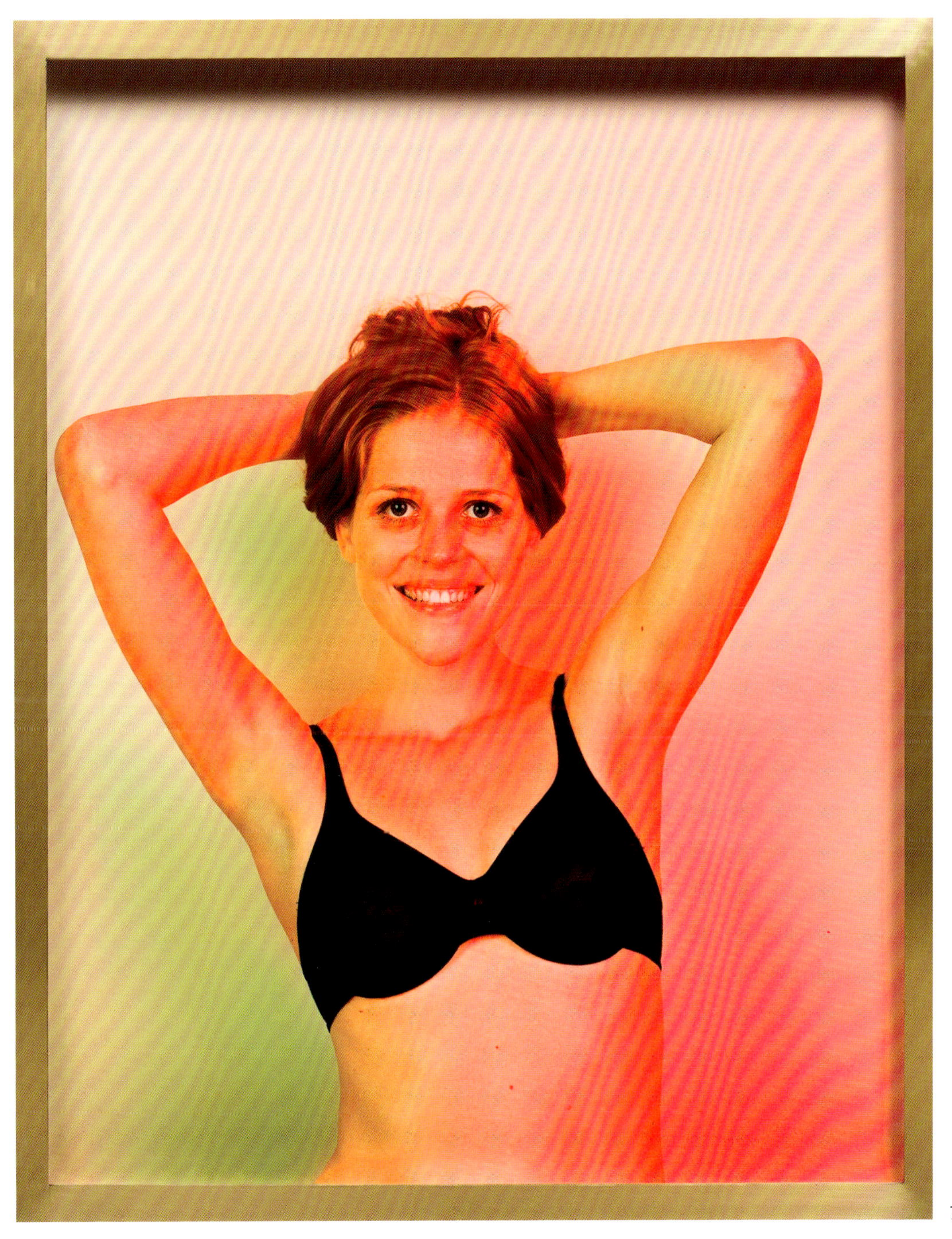

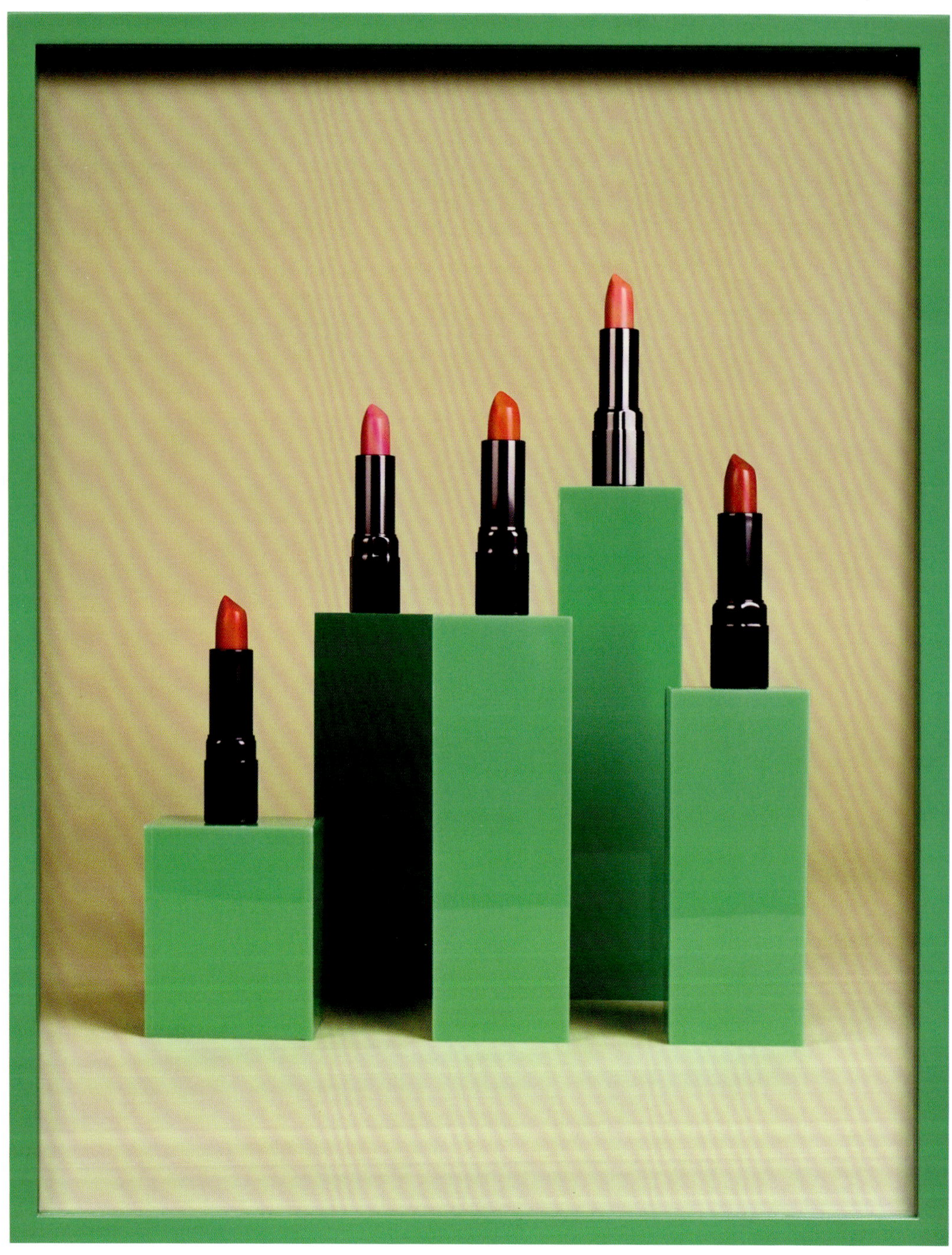

19. Elad Lassry
*Lipstick*, 2009
C-print
14 x 11 inches

20. Elad Lassry
*Selkirk Rex, LaPerm*, 2011
C-print, diptych, edition 4 of 5
14 ½ x 11 ½ inches (each)

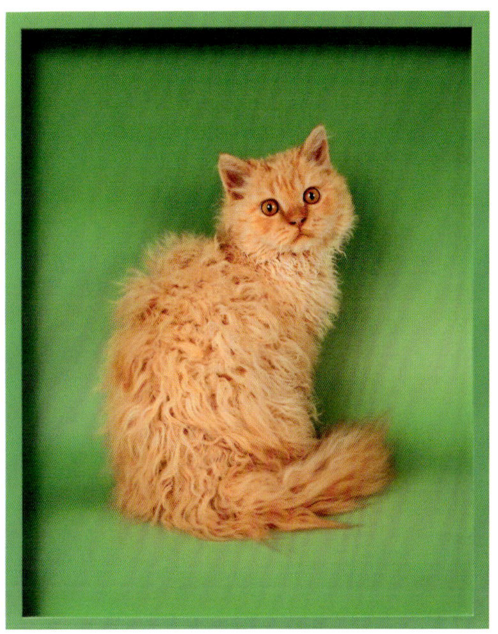

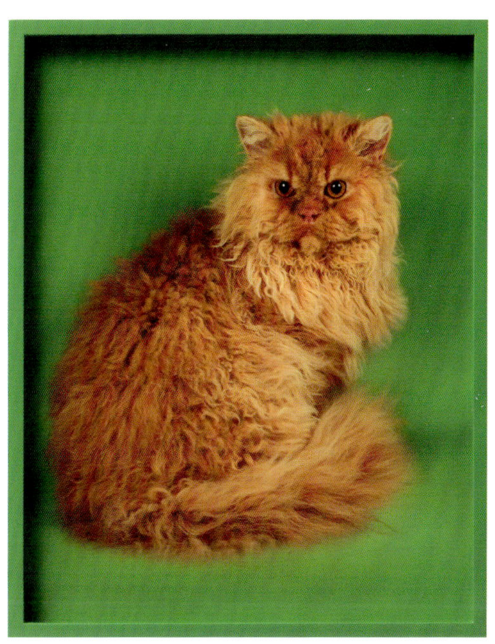

21. Steven Baldi
*Branded Light (Fuji-Canon)*,
2016
Gelatin silver print,
edition of 3
11 x 8 ¾ inches

22. Steven Baldi
*Branded Light (Leica-Nikon)*,
2016
Gelatin silver print,
edition of 3
11 x 8 ¾ inches

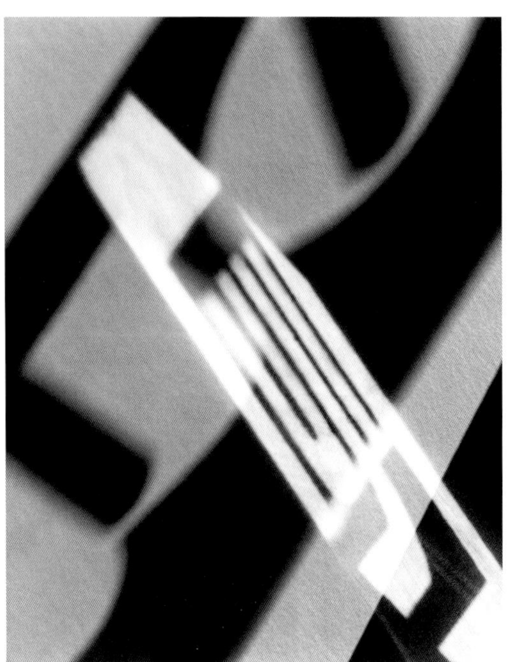

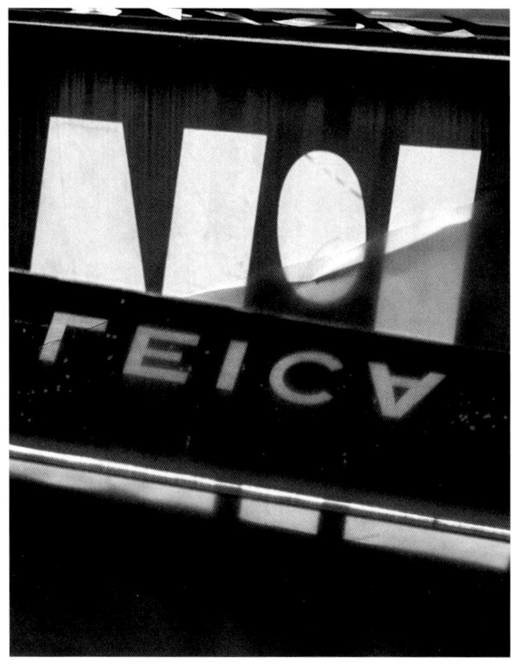


23. Steven Baldi
*Branded Light (Canon)*, 2016
Gelatin silver print,
edition of 3
8 ¾ x 11 inches

24. Steven Baldi
*Branded Light (Zeiss)*, 2016
Gelatin silver print,
edition of 3
8 ¾ x 11 inches

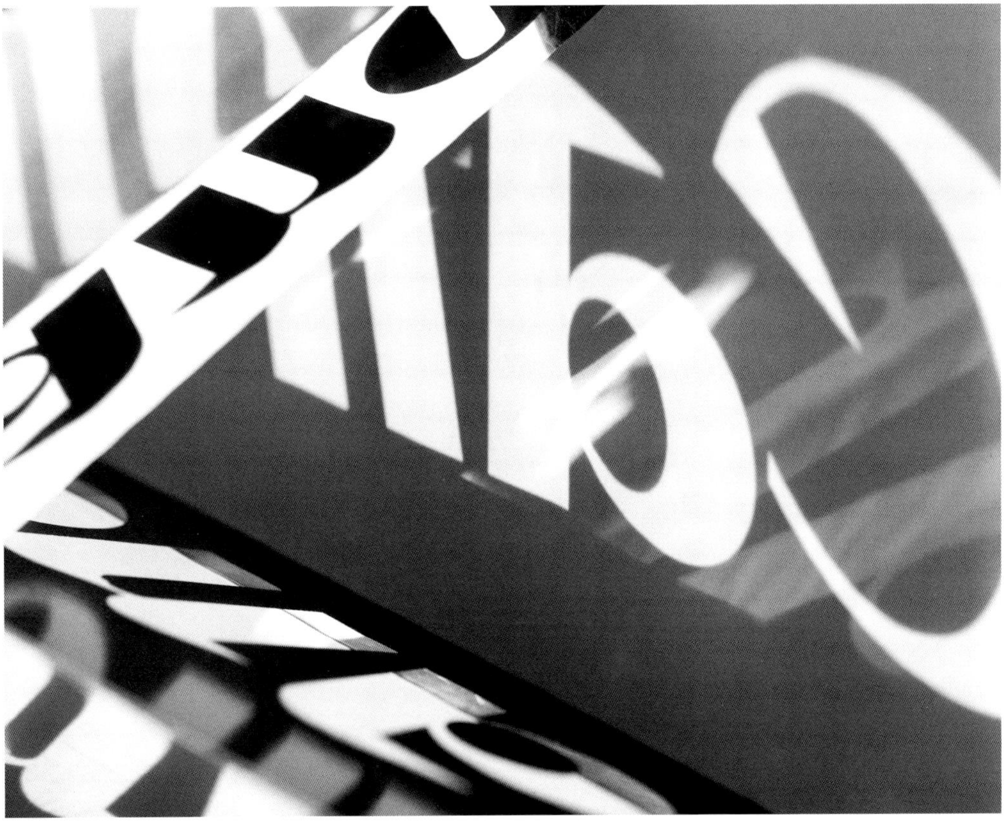

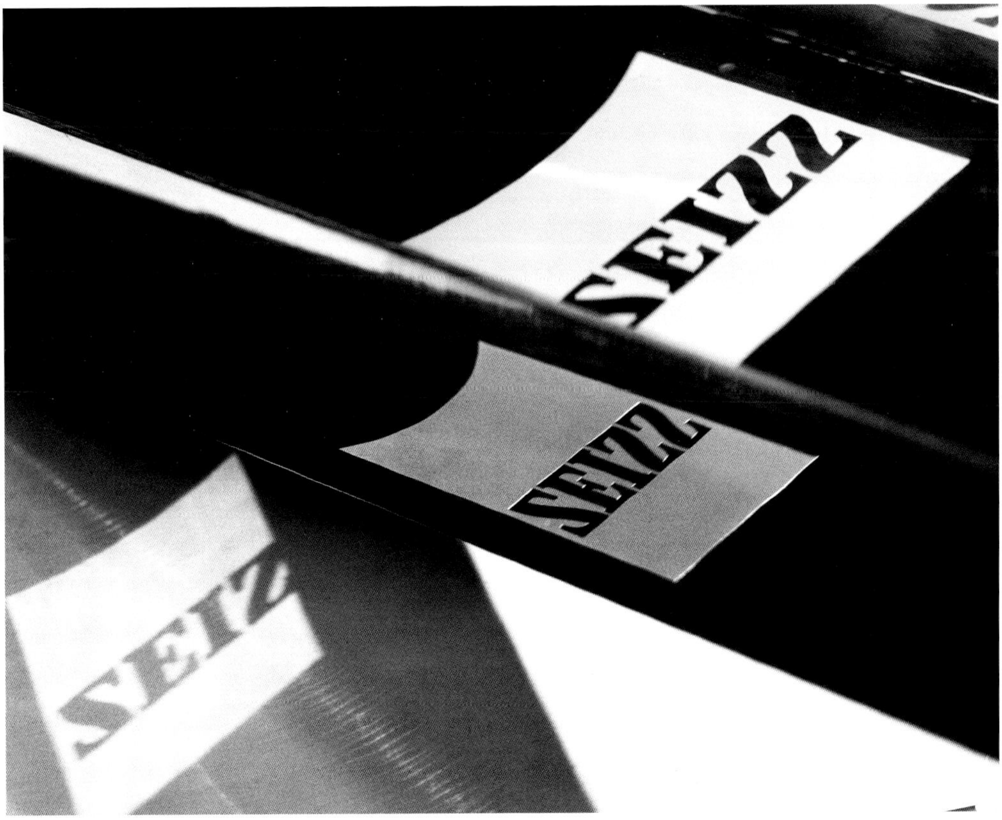

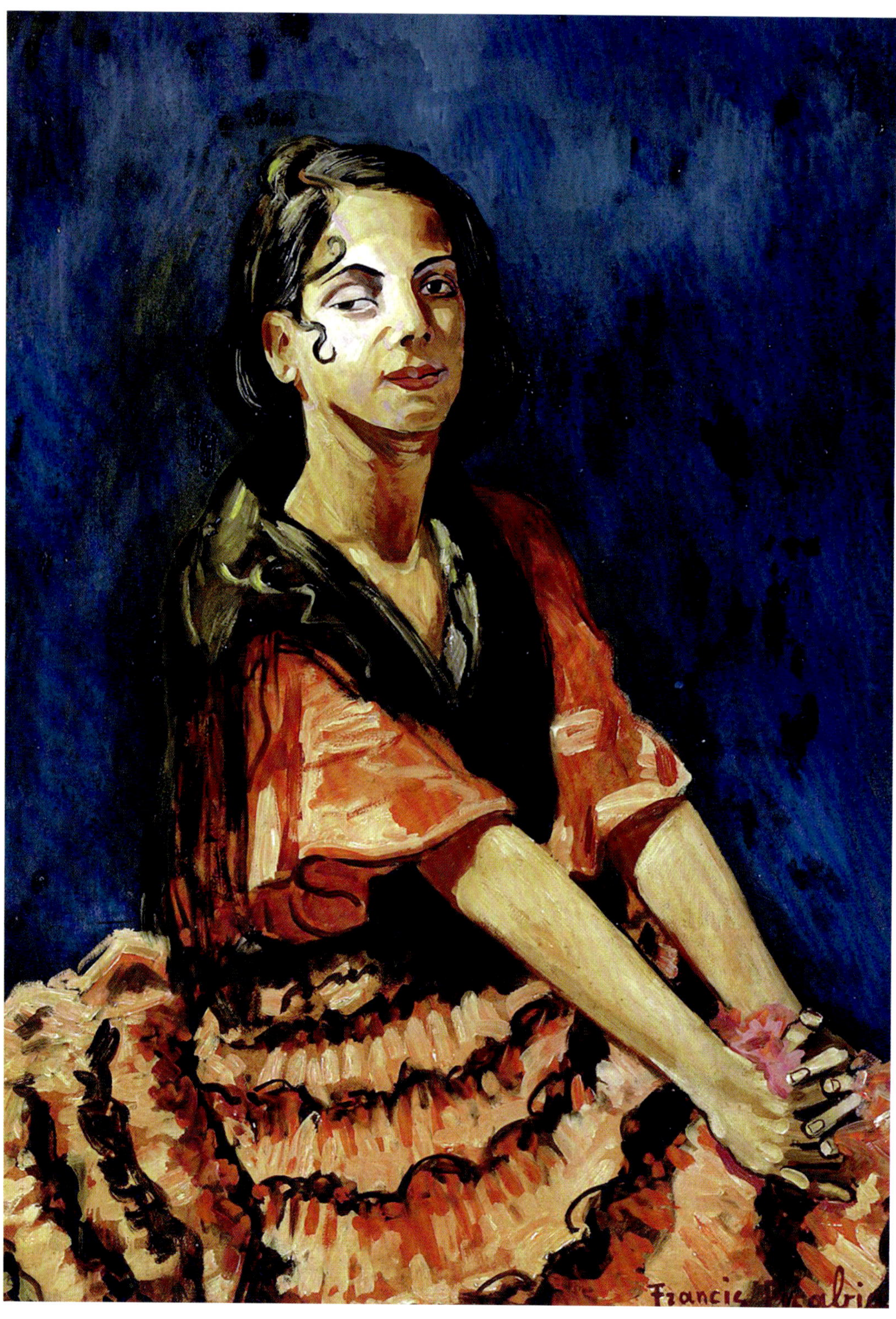

25. Francis Picabia
*L'Andalusia*, ca. 1941–42
Oil on canvas
41 ¾ x 29 ⅞ inches

26. Francis Picabia
*Don Quichotte*, ca. 1941–42
Oil and ink on cardboard
37 ¾ x 29 ⅞ inches

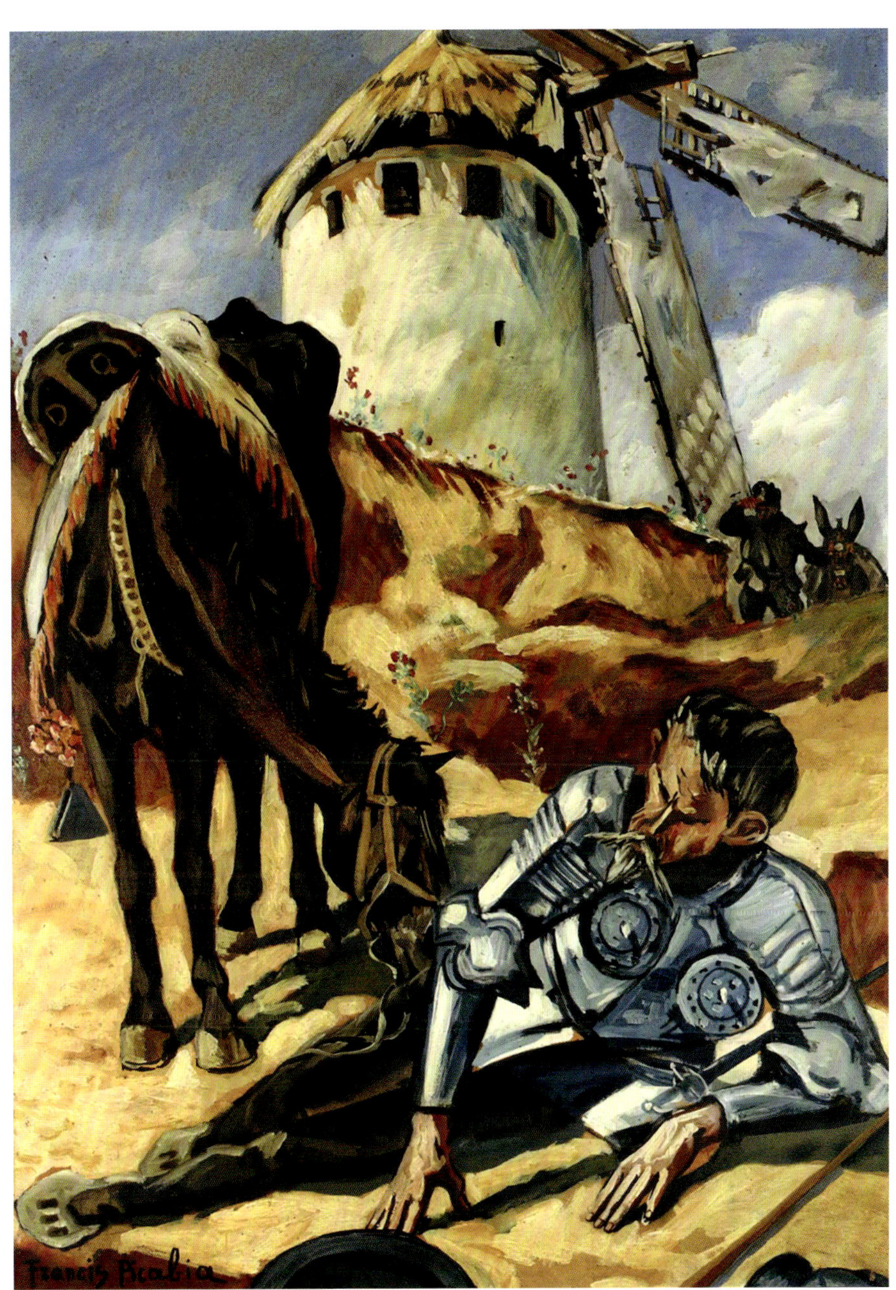

27. Julian Schnabel
*Veramente Bestia V*
*(Girl with No Eyes)*, 1988
Oil on found object
19 ¾ x 15 ¾ inches

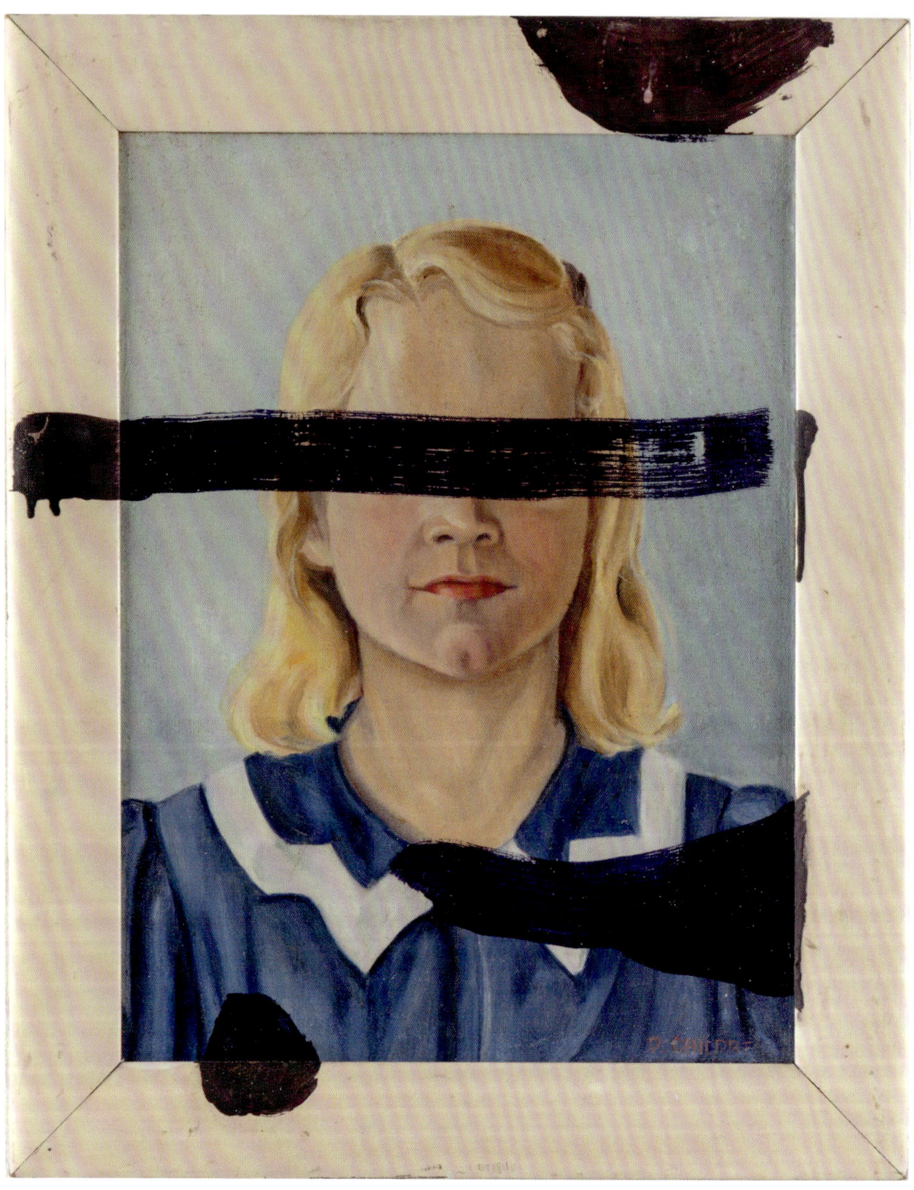

28. Tom Scicluna
*Ordinance No. C-14-23*, 2014
Neon sign and fixtures
20 x 37 x 3 inches

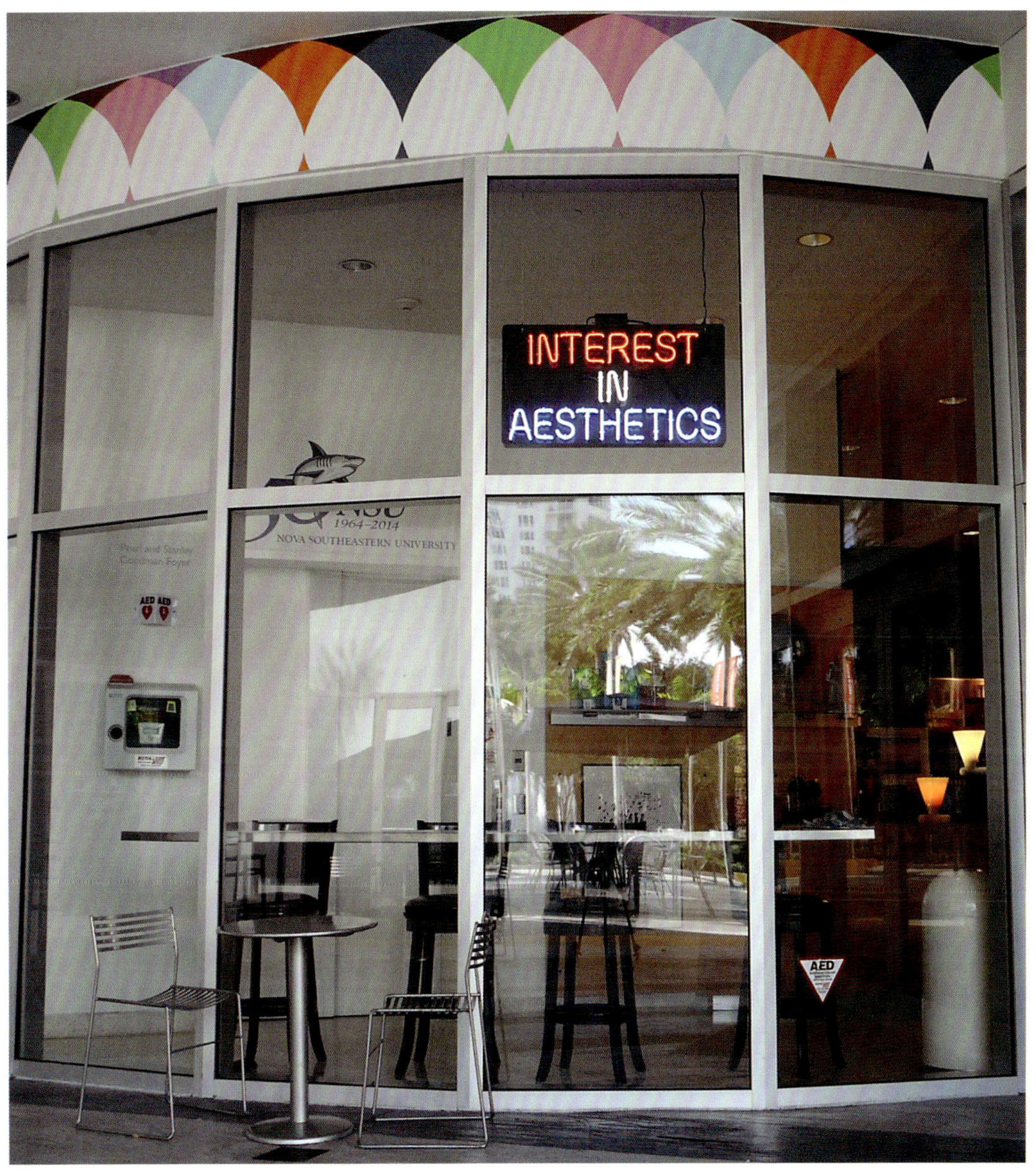

29. Claire Fontaine
*Jurors*, 2013
Lightbox and digital print
on vinyl
104 5/16 x 165 3/8 x 6 5/16 inches

***Jurors (Art)***

Jurors are always apt to be wrong. The only argument in favor of this jury is that the three differed in their selection of the first, second and third prizes, showing how close the decision was. But even the conviction of having been fair does not change my doubts on the right to judge at all.

Statement published in the catalog of the Bel-Ami International Competition and Exhibition 1946–47: *The Temptation of St. Anthony* (Washington: The American Federation of Arts), p. 3.

30. John Baldessari
Detail from the Artist's Book
*Choosing: Green Beans*, 1972
Offset lithograph on paper
11 ¾ x 8 ¼ x ¼ inches

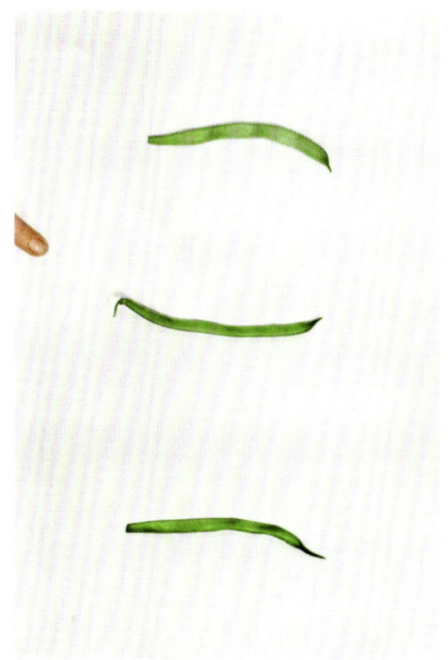

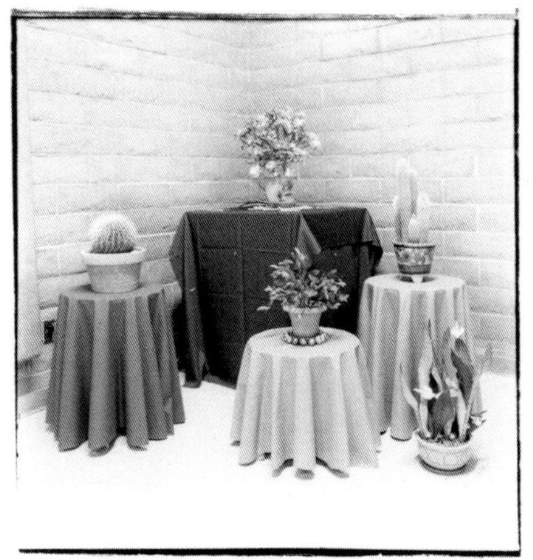

31. Judy Fiskin
Plate 138, from *Some Aesthetic Decisions*, 1990
Gelatin silver print
8 x 5 ¾ inches

32. Judy Fiskin
Plate 140, from *Some Aesthetic Decisions*, 1990
Gelatin silver print
8 x 5 ¾ inches

33. Judy Fiskin
Plate 155, from *Some Aesthetic Decisions*, 1990
Gelatin silver print
8 x 5 ¾ inches

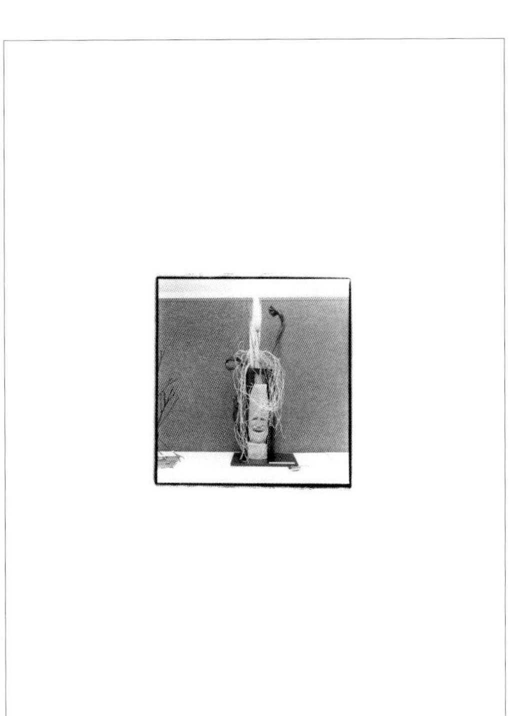

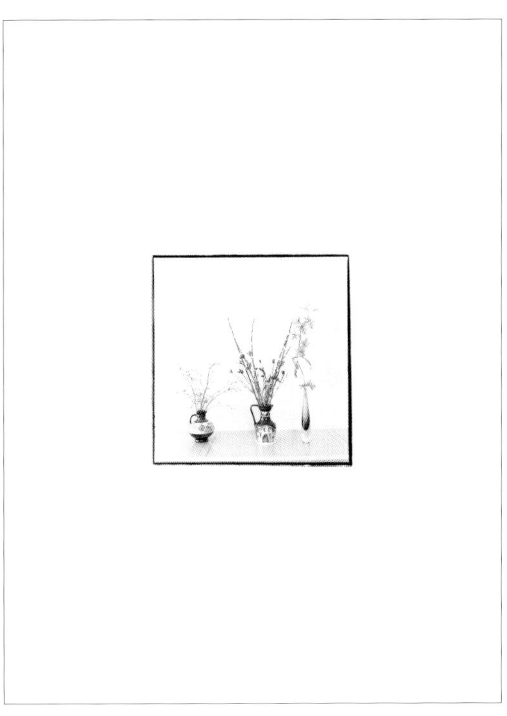

34. Judy Fiskin
Plate 162, from *Some Aesthetic Decisions*, 1990
Gelatin silver print
8 x 5 ¾ inches

35. Judy Fiskin
Plate 164, from *Some Aesthetic Decisions*, 1990
Gelatin silver print
8 x 5 ¾ inches

36. Judy Fiskin
Plate 251, from *Some Art*, 1990
Gelatin silver print
8 x 5 $\frac{7}{16}$ inches

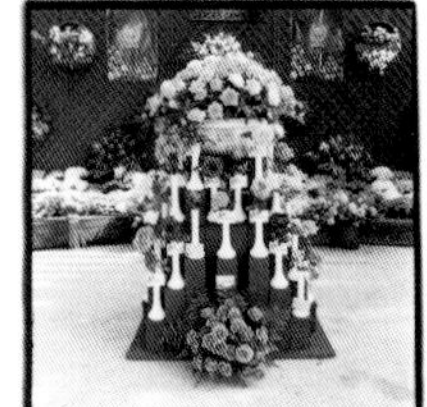

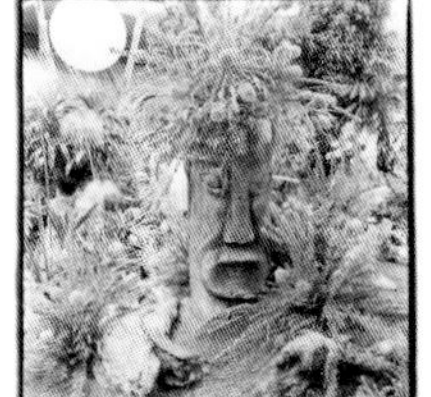

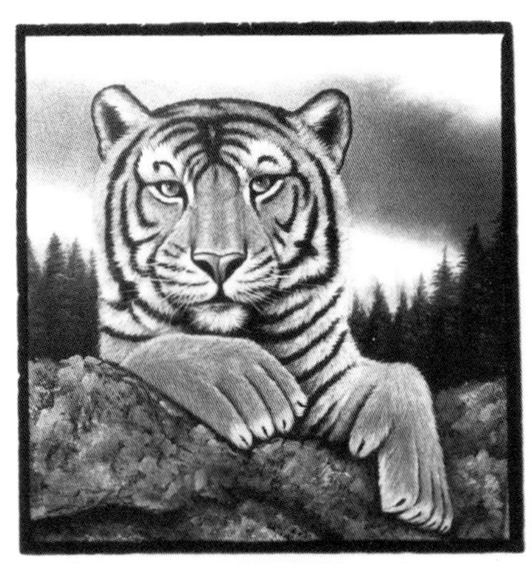

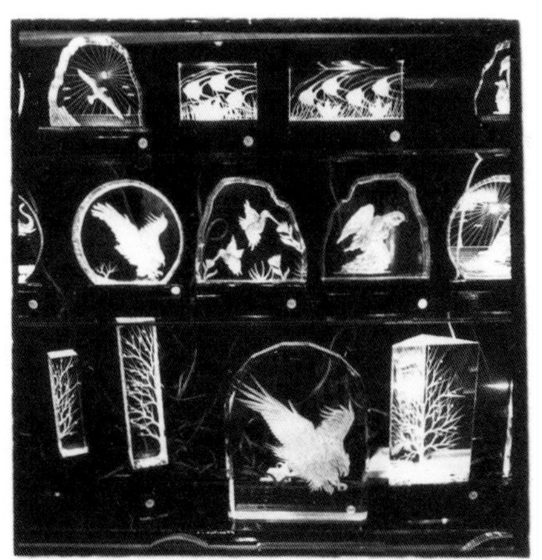

37. Judy Fiskin
Plate 254, from *Some Art*,
1990
Gelatin silver print
8 x 5 7/16 inches

38. Judy Fiskin
Plate 263, from *Some Art*,
1990
Gelatin silver print
8 x 5 7/16 inches

39. Judy Fiskin
Plate 269, from *Some Art*,
1990
Gelatin silver print
8 x 5 7/16 inches

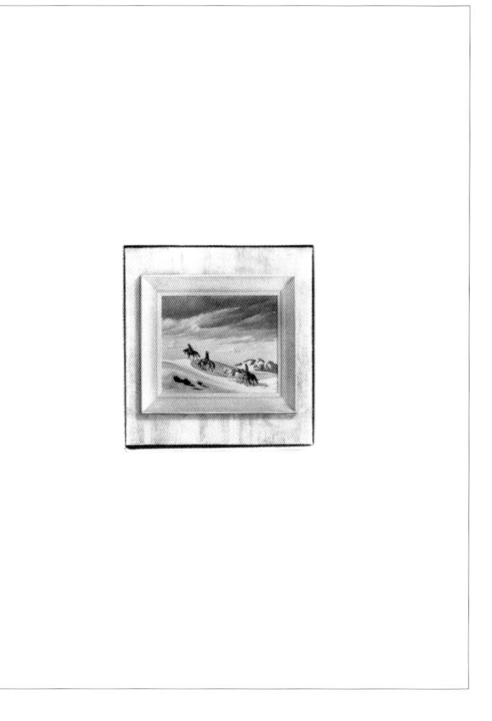

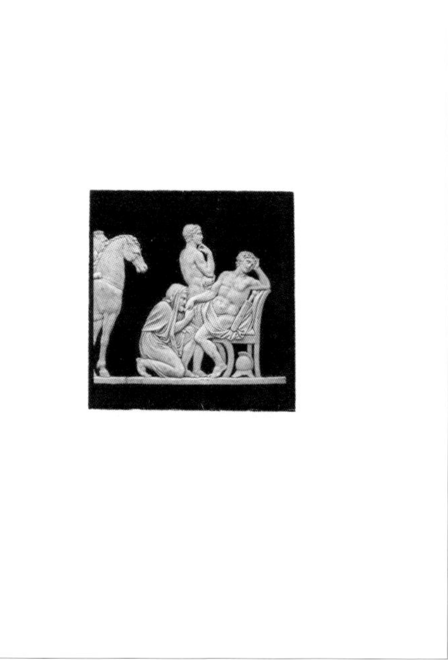

40. Judy Fiskin
*50 Ways to Set the Table*, 2003
Video
26 minutes, 31 seconds

41. Bernd and Hilla Becher
*Water Towers*, 1980
Gelatin silver prints (9)
61 ¼ x 49 ¼ inches overall

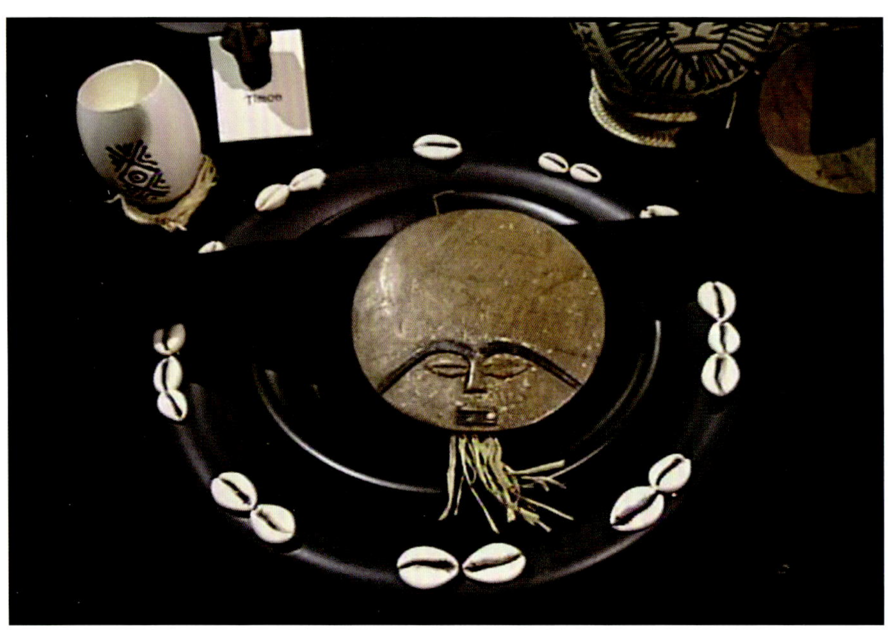

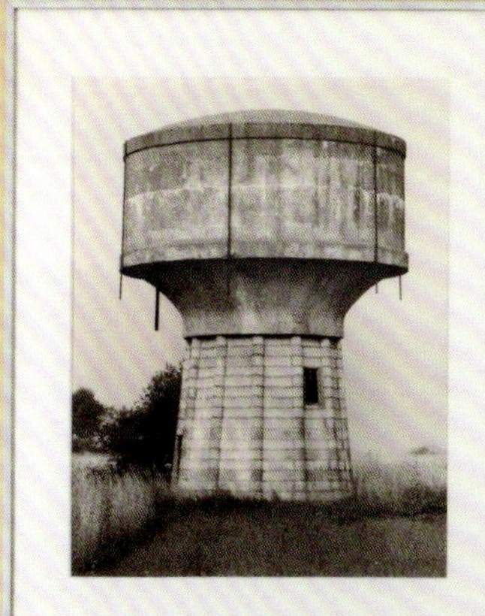
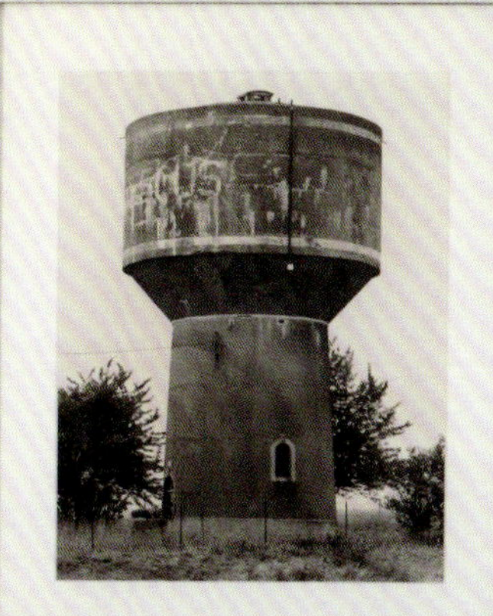
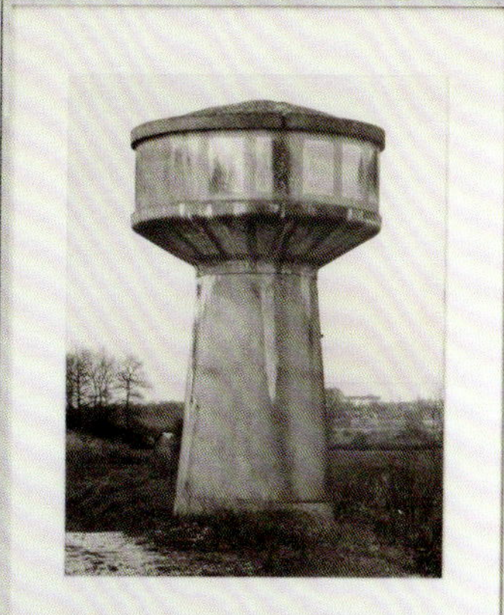
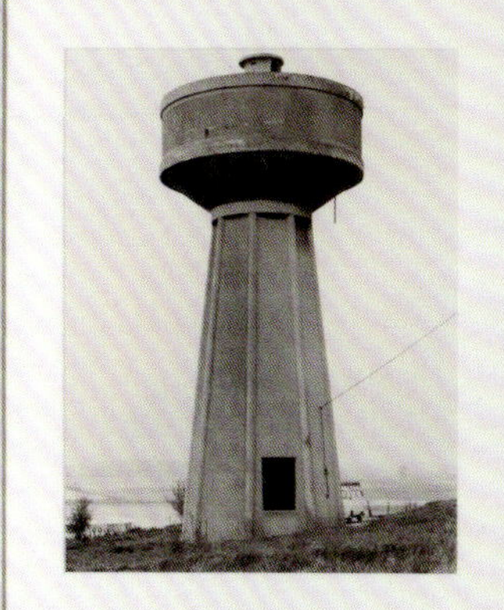
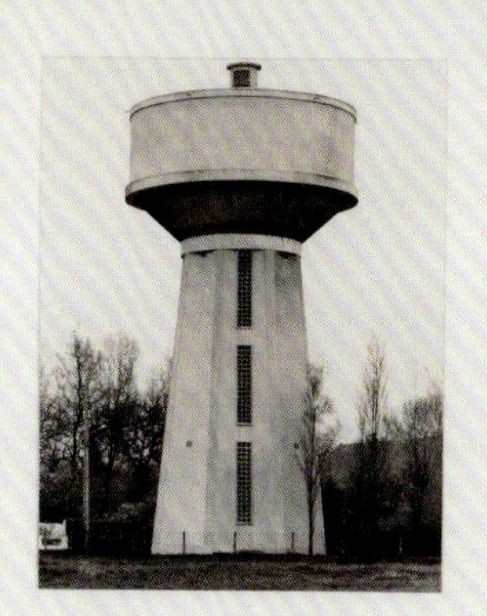
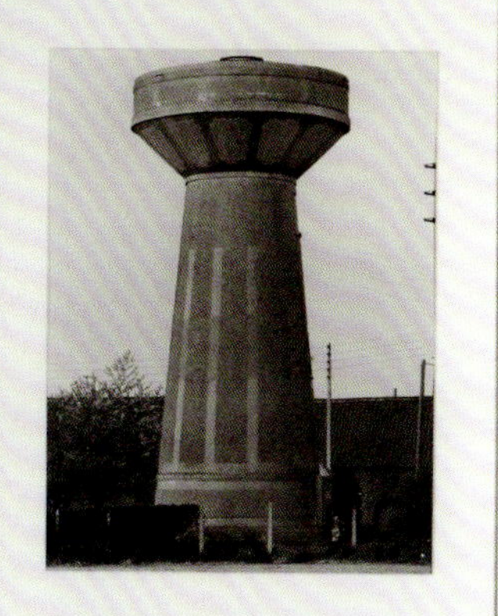
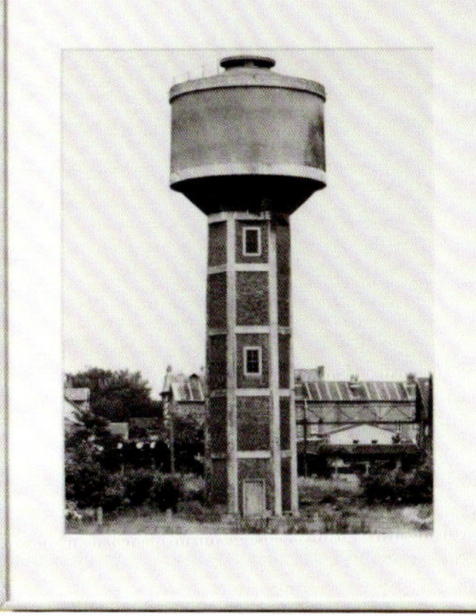
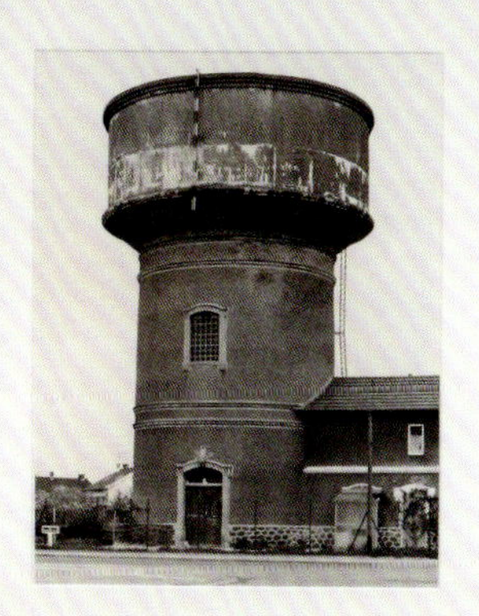
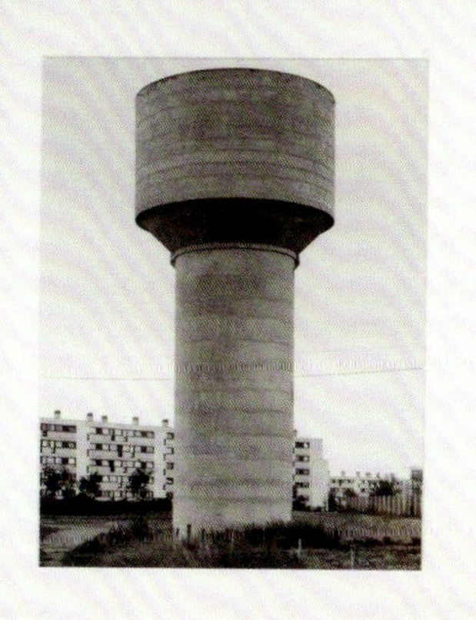

42. Sophie Calle
*Blind Series*, 1986
Photographs and text panels

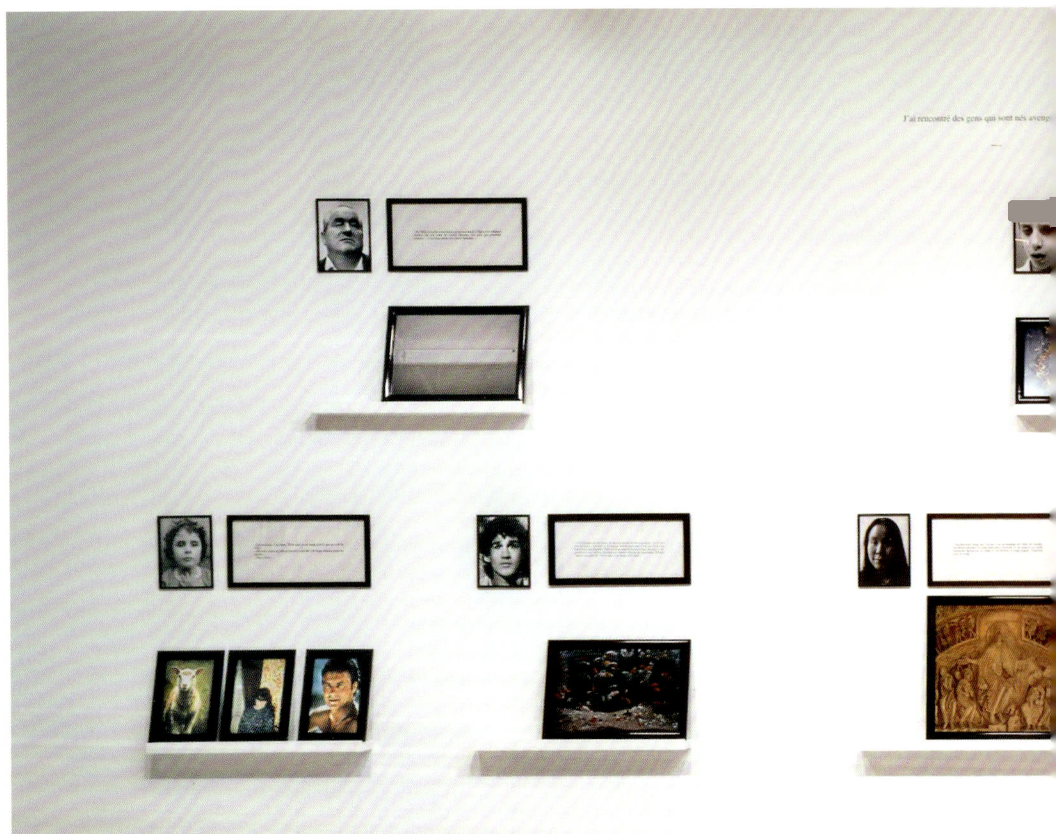

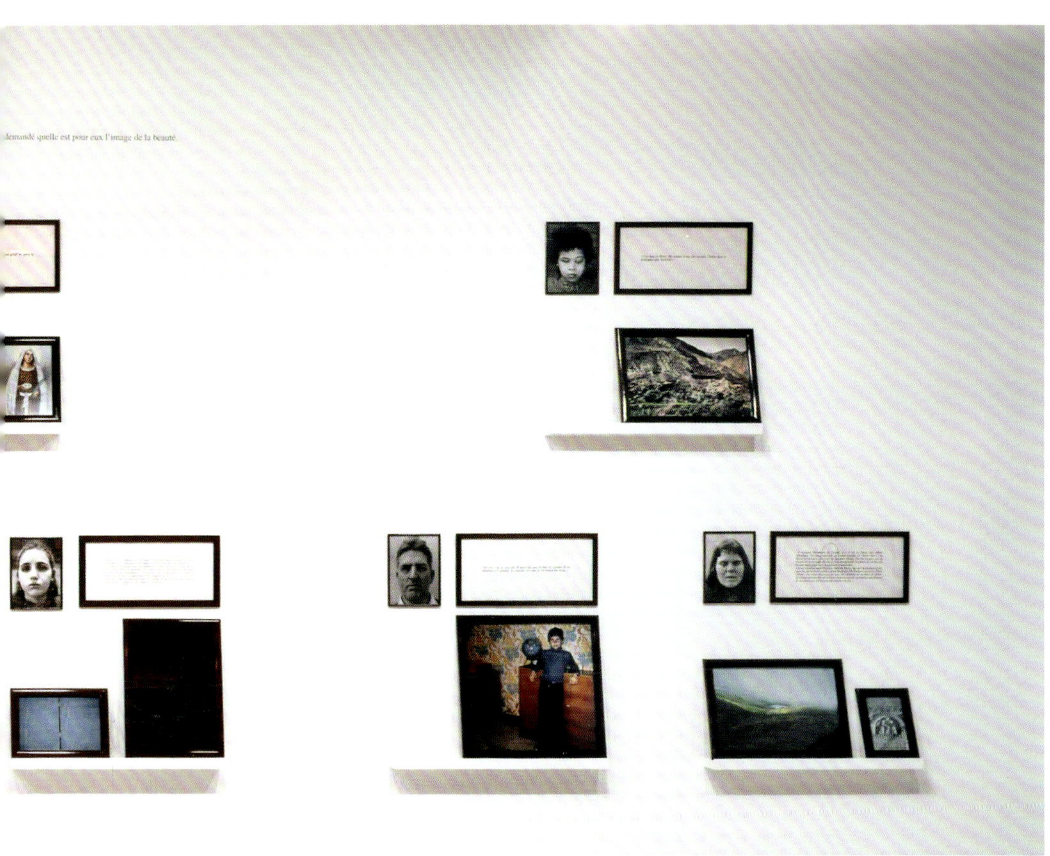
demandé quelle est pour eux l'image de la beauté.

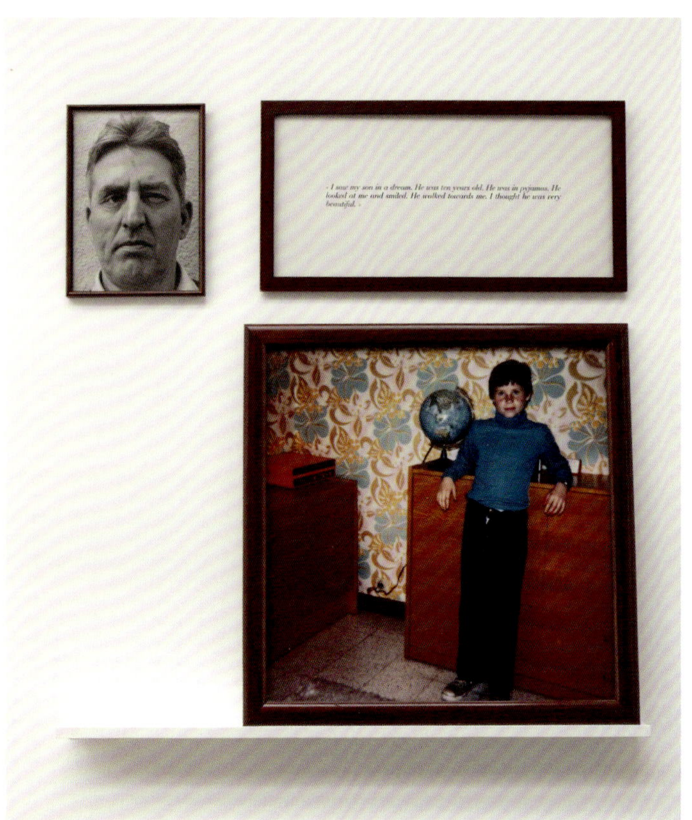


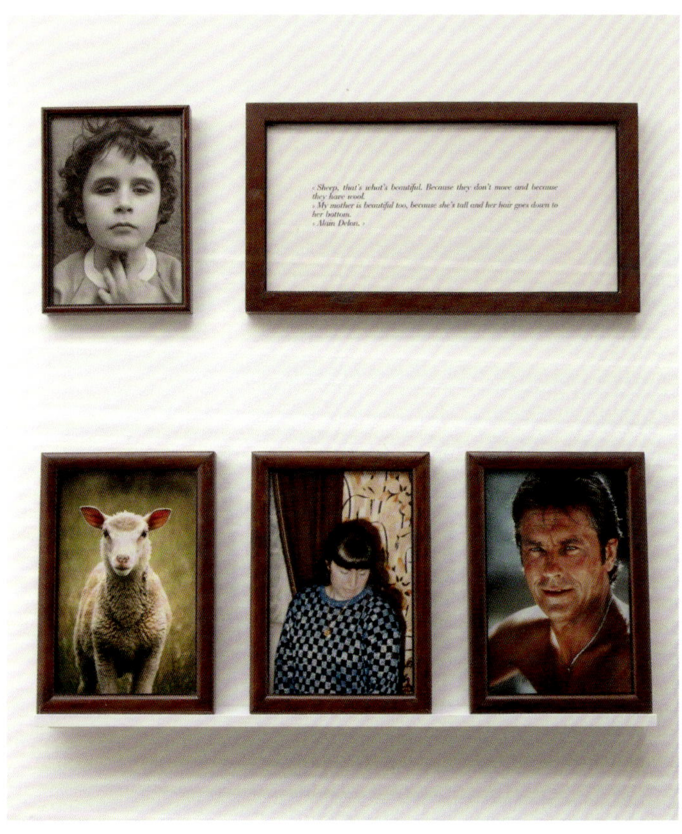


43, 44. Sophie Calle
*Blind Series*, 1986
Photographs and text panels

45. Komar and Melamid
*The People's Choice*, 1995
Silkscreen on paper (6)
26 ½ x 19 inches

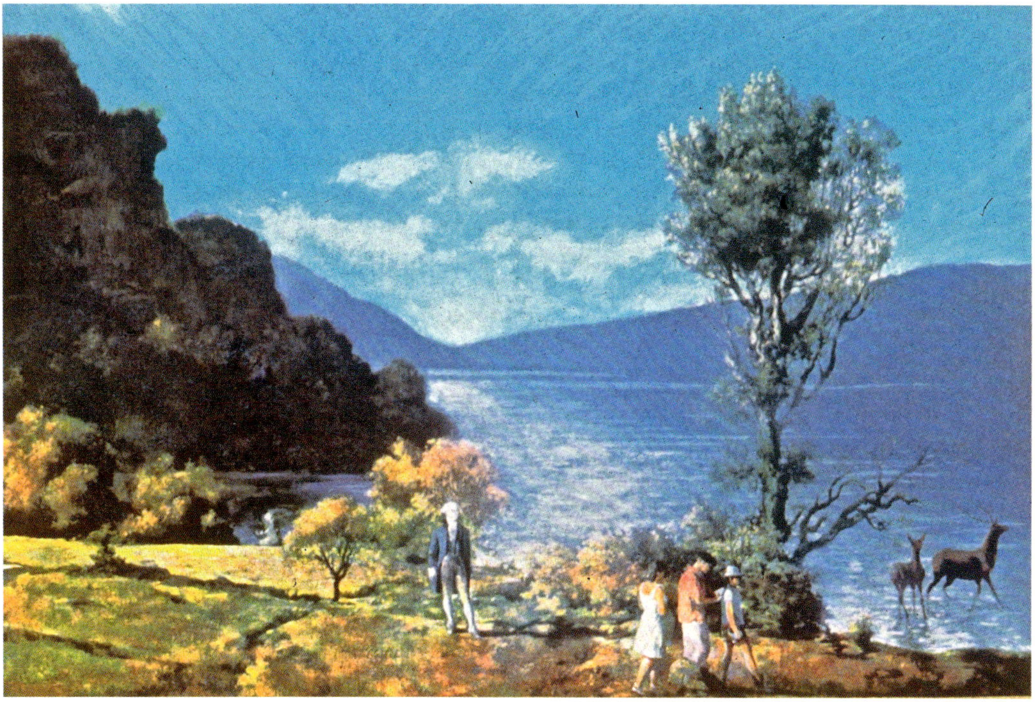

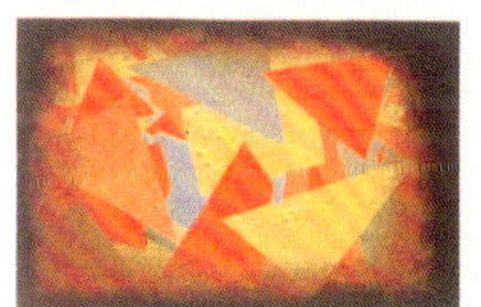

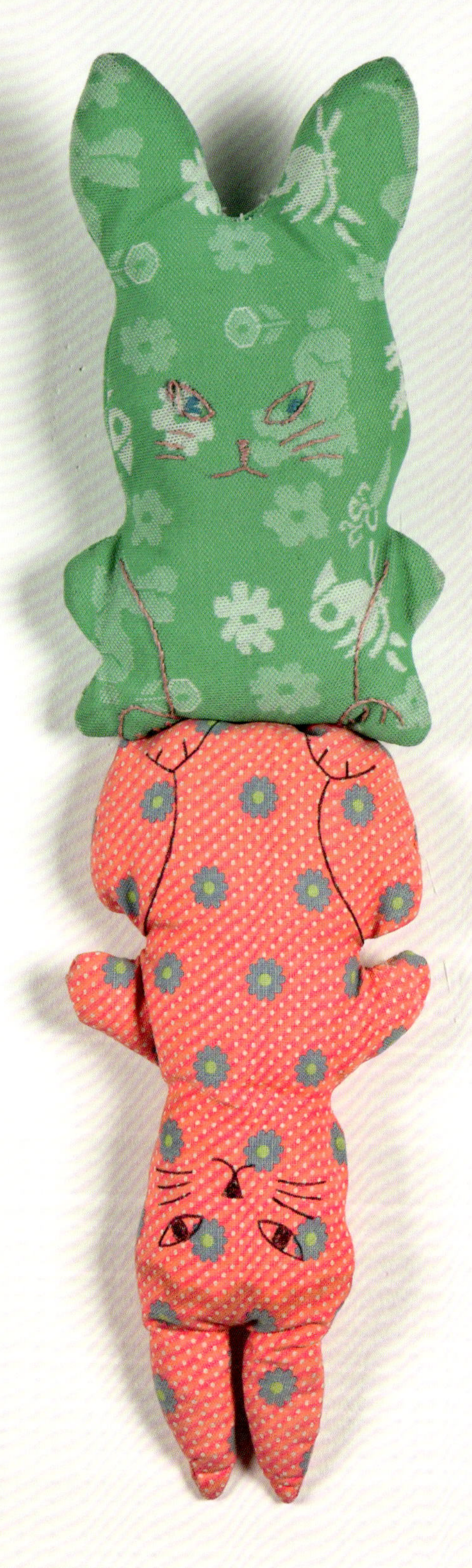

46. Mike Kelley
*Pink Shadow*, 1989
Fabric, thread, ink, and stuffing
18 x 5 ¼ x 2 ⅜ inches

47. Kara Walker
*Untitled*, 1994
Paper on canvas
10 x 10 x ¾ inches

48. Kara Walker
*Untitled*, 1994
Paper on canvas
10 x 10 x ¾ inches

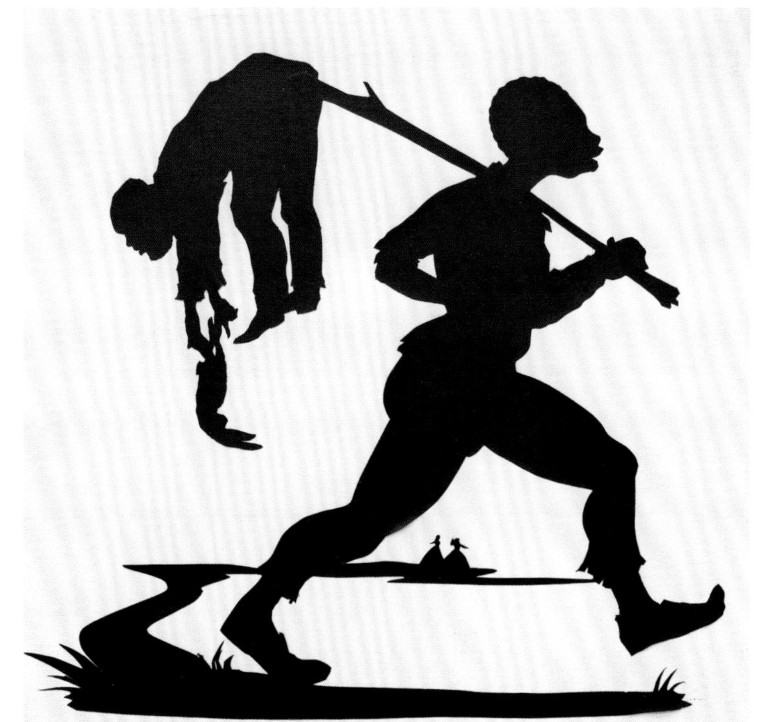

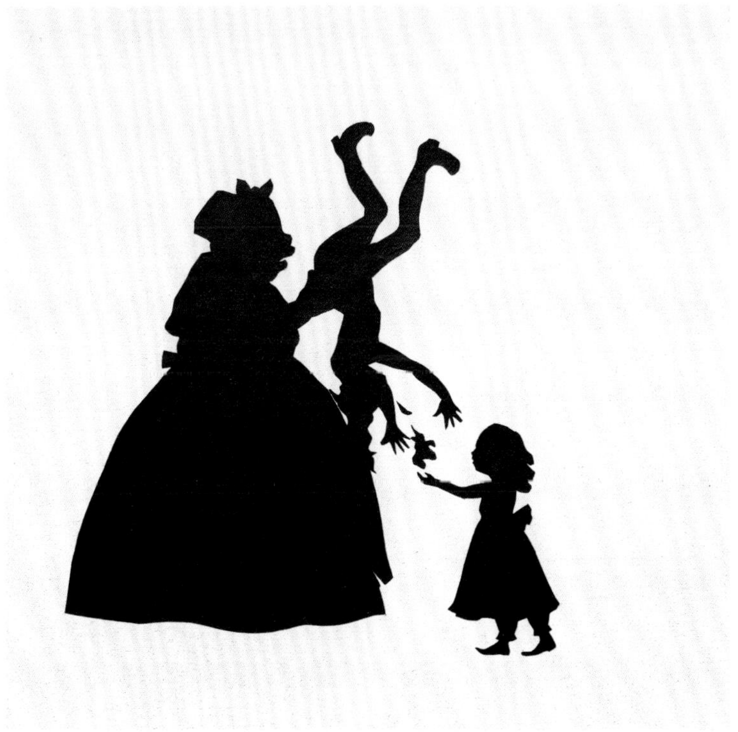

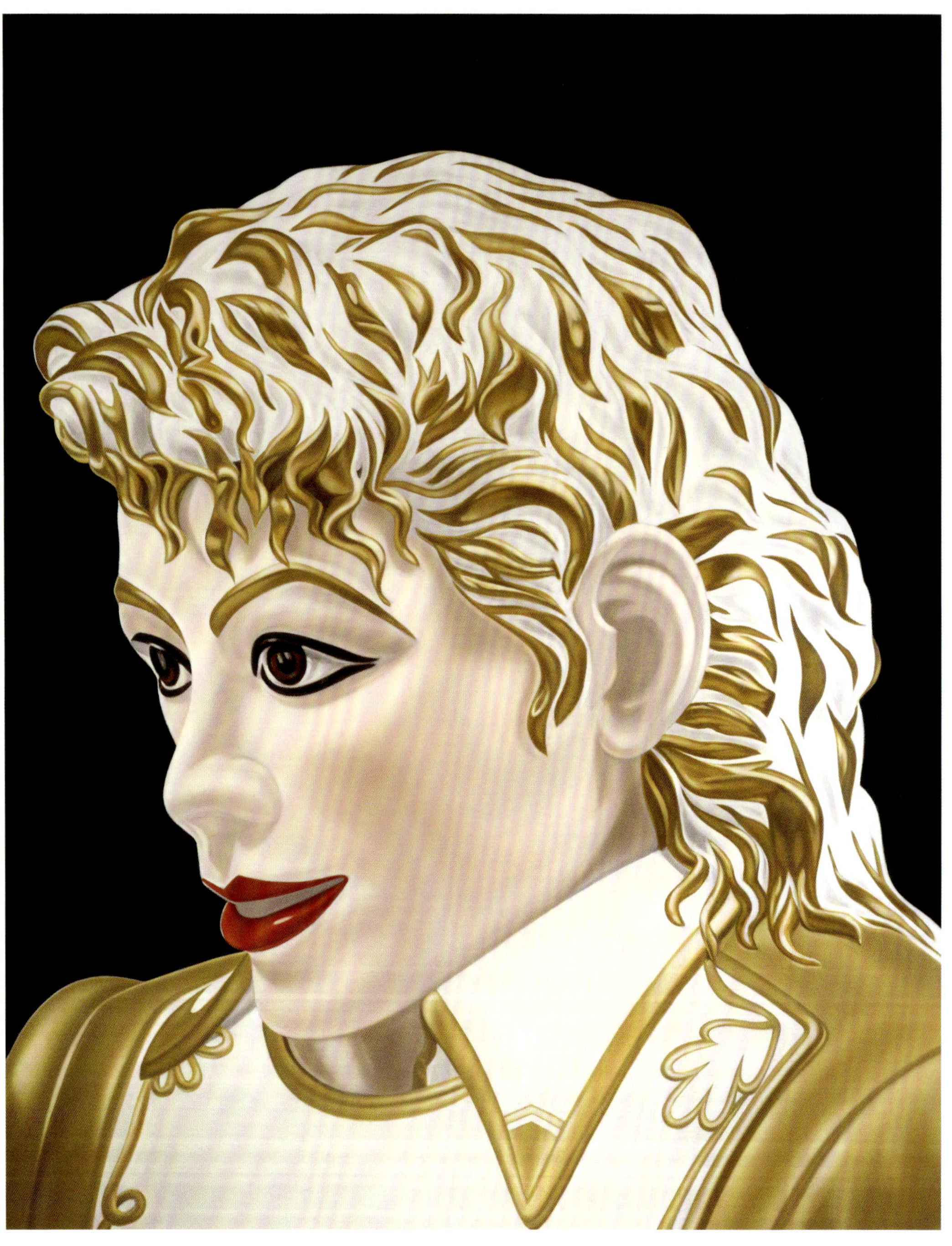

49. Richard Phillips
*Jacko (after Jeff Koons)*, 1998
Oil on linen
99 x 78 x 3 inches

50. Richard Phillips
*Fiktive Models I*, 2016
Oil on linen
108 x 73 ⅛ inches

51. Richard Phillips
*Fiktive Models IV*, 2016
Oil on linen
108 x 72 inches

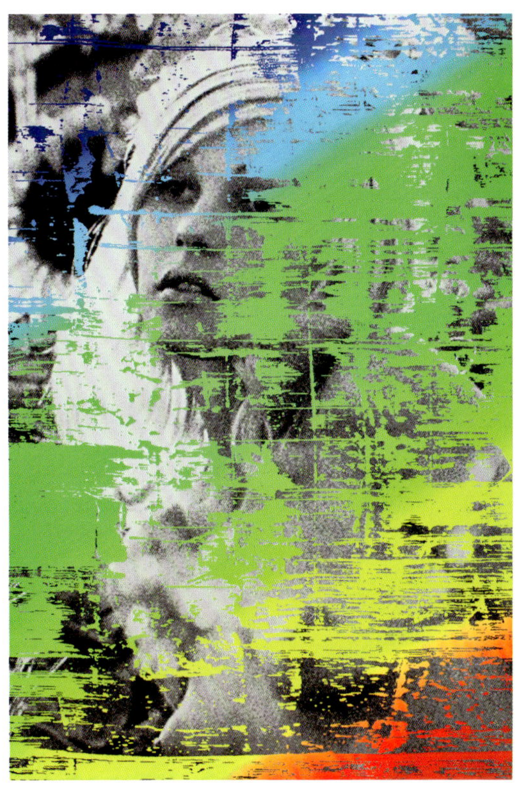

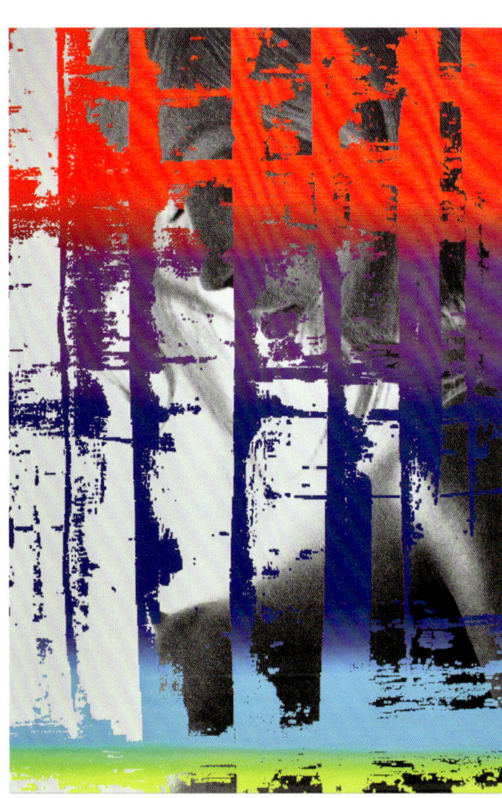

52. Samson Kambalu
*Runner*, 2014
Digital color video,
edition of 3 plus 1 AP
50 seconds

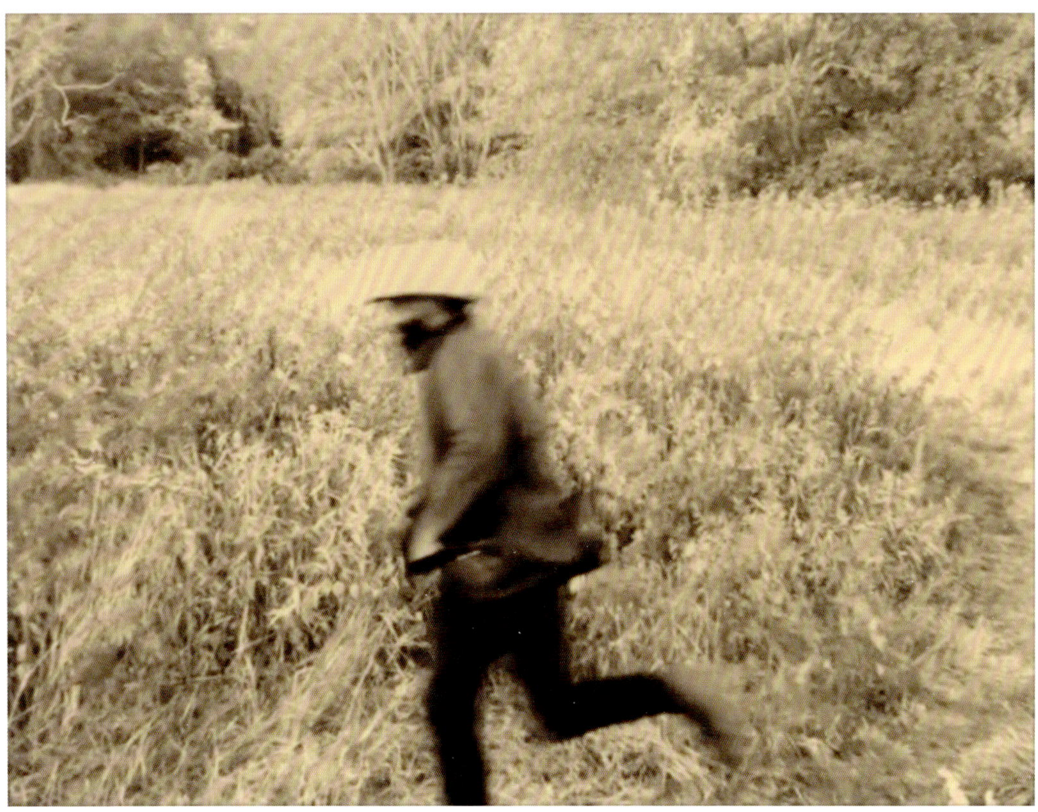

# Works in the Exhibition

Cory Arcangel (American; b. 1978, Buffalo, NY; lives and works in Brooklyn, NY)
*Apple GarageBand Auto Tune Demonstration*, 2007
Film projection from a digital source
8 minutes, 48 seconds
Courtesy Cory Arcangel and Team (Gallery, Inc.)
(pl. 16)

John Baldessari (American; b. 1931, National City, CA; lives and works in Los Angeles and Venice, CA)
*Choosing: Green Beans*, 1972
Offset lithograph on paper
11 ³⁄₄ x 8 ¹⁄₄ x ¹⁄₄ inches
Rosemary Furtak Collection, Walker Art Center Library
(pl. 30)

Steven Baldi (American; b. 1983, Huntington Beach, CA; lives and works in Los Angeles, CA)
*Branded Light (Fuji-Canon)*, 2016
Gelatin silver print, edition of 3
11 x 8 ³⁄₄ inches
Courtesy the artist and Koenig & Clinton, New York
(pl. 21)

Steven Baldi (American; b. 1983, Huntington Beach, CA; lives and works in Los Angeles, CA)
*Branded Light (Leica-Nikon)*, 2016
Gelatin silver print, edition of 3
11 x 8 ³⁄₄ inches
Courtesy the artist and Koenig & Clinton, New York
(pl. 22)

Steven Baldi (American; b. 1983, Huntington Beach, CA; lives and works in Los Angeles, CA)
*Branded Light (Canon)*, 2016
Gelatin silver print, edition of 3
8 ³⁄₄ x 11 inches
Courtesy the artist and Koenig & Clinton, New York
(pl. 23)

Steven Baldi (American; b. 1983, Huntington Beach, CA; lives and works in Los Angeles, CA)
*Branded Light (Zeiss)*, 2016
Gelatin silver print, edition of 3
8 ³⁄₄ x 11 inches
Courtesy the artist and Koenig & Clinton, New York
(pl. 24)

Bernd and Hilla Becher (German; 1931–2007, German; 1934–2015)
*Water Towers*, 1980
Gelatin silver prints (9)
61 ¹⁄₄ x 49 ¹⁄₄ inches overall
Rosalind and Melvin Jacobs Collection, New York
(pl. 41)

Mike Bidlo (American; b. 1953, Chicago, IL; lives and works in New York, NY)
*Fractured Fountain (Not Duchamp Fountain 1917)*, 2015
Bronze, edition of 8
14 ³⁄₄ x 16 x 11 inches
Francis M. Naumann Fine Art, New York
(pl. 6)

Sophie Calle (French; b. 1953, Paris, France; lives and works in Malakoff, France)
*Blind Series*, 1986
Photographs and text panels
Collection of Stuart and Judy Spence, Los Angeles
(pls. 42–44)

Marcel Duchamp (French; 1887–1968)
*La Boîte verte. La Mariée mise à nu par ses célibataires, même (The Green Box. The Bride Stripped Bare by Her Bachelors, Even)*, 1934
Cardboard and paper
13 5/8 x 11 3/4 x 1 3/8 inches
Collection of The John and Mable Ringling Museum of Art, the State Art Museum of Florida, Florida State University, Sarasota, FL
(not reproduced)

Marcel Duchamp (French; 1887–1968)
*Boîte-en-valise (De ou par Marcel Duchamp ou Rrose Sélavy) (The Box in a Valise [Of or by Marcel Duchamp or Rrose Sélavy])*, 1941/1961
Leather valise containing miniature replicas
Mixed media, edition 1 of 30
16 x 15 x 4 inches
Collection of Pérez Art Museum Miami, Museum purchase with funds provided by Lang Baumgarten and Mimi Floback and Sally Ashton Story in memory of Jon Ashton
(pl. 2)

Marcel Duchamp (French; 1887–1968)
*Trébuchet (Trap)*, 1917, 1964
Wood and metal, edition of 7
7 3/8 x 39 3/8 x 4 7/8 inches
Collection of The John and Mable Ringling Museum of Art, the State Art Museum of Florida, Florida State University, Sarasota, Florida
(pl. 3)

Judy Fiskin (American; b. 1945, Chicago, IL; lives and works in Los Angeles, CA)
Plate 138, from *Some Aesthetic Decisions*, 1990
Gelatin silver print
8 x 5 3/4 inches
Courtesy of Richard Telles Fine Art, Los Angeles
(pl. 31)

Judy Fiskin (American; b. 1945, Chicago, IL; lives and works in Los Angeles, CA)
Plate 140, from *Some Aesthetic Decisions*, 1990
Gelatin silver print
8 x 5 3/4 inches
Courtesy of Richard Telles Fine Art, Los Angeles
(pl. 32)

Judy Fiskin (American; b. 1945, Chicago, IL; lives and works in Los Angeles, CA)
Plate 155, from *Some Aesthetic Decisions*, 1990
Gelatin silver print
8 x 5 3/4 inches
Courtesy of Richard Telles Fine Art, Los Angeles
(pl. 33)

Judy Fiskin (American; b. 1945, Chicago, IL; lives and works in Los Angeles, CA)
Plate 162, from *Some Aesthetic Decisions*, 1990
Gelatin silver print
8 x 5 3/4 inches
Courtesy of Richard Telles Fine Art, Los Angeles
(pl. 34)

Judy Fiskin (American; b. 1945, Chicago, IL; lives and works in Los Angeles, CA)
Plate 164, from *Some Aesthetic Decisions*, 1990
Gelatin silver print
8 x 5 3/4 inches
Courtesy of Richard Telles Fine Art, Los Angeles
(pl. 35)

Judy Fiskin (American; b. 1945, Chicago, IL; lives and works in Los Angeles, CA)
Plate 251, from *Some Art*, 1990
Gelatin silver print
8 x 5 7/16 inches
Courtesy of Richard Telles Fine Art, Los Angeles
(pl. 36)

Judy Fiskin (American; b. 1945, Chicago, IL; lives and works in Los Angeles, CA)
Plate 254, from *Some Art*, 1990
Gelatin silver print
8 x 5 7/16 inches
Courtesy of Richard Telles Fine Art, Los Angeles
(pl. 37)

Judy Fiskin (American; b. 1945, Chicago, IL; lives and works in Los Angeles, CA)
Plate 263, from *Some Art*, 1990
Gelatin silver print
8 x 5 7/16 inches
Courtesy of Richard Telles Fine Art, Los Angeles
(pl. 38)

Judy Fiskin (American; b. 1945, Chicago, IL; lives and works in Los Angeles, CA)
Plate 269, from *Some Art*, 1990
Gelatin silver print
8 x 5 7/16 inches
Courtesy of Richard Telles Fine Art, Los Angeles
(pl. 39)

Judy Fiskin (American; b. 1945, Chicago, IL; lives and works in Los Angeles, CA)
*50 Ways to Set the Table*, 2003
Video
26 minutes, 31 seconds
Courtesy of Richard Telles Fine Art, Los Angeles
(pl. 40)

Claire Fontaine (French artist collective, founded in 2004 in Paris, France, and based in Paris, France)
*Jurors*, 2013
Lightbox and digital print on vinyl
104 5/16 x 165 3/8 x 6 5/16 inches
NSU Art Museum Fort Lauderdale; purchased with funds provided by Michael and Diane Bienes by exchange
(pl. 29)

Samson Kambalu (Malawi, Africa; b. 1975, lives and works in London, England)
*Runner*, 2014
Digital color video, edition of 3 plus 1 AP
50 seconds
NSU Art Museum Fort Lauderdale; purchased with funds provided by Michael and Diane Bienes by exchange
(pl. 52)

Mike Kelley (American; 1954–2012)
*Pink Shadow*, 1989
Fabric, thread, ink, and stuffing
18 x 5 1/4 x 2 3/8 inches
Rubell Family Collection, Miami
(pl. 46)

Mike Kelley (American; 1954–2012)
*Rewrite*, 1995
Enamel on wood
96 1/8 x 47 7/8 inches
Rubell Family Collection, Miami
(not reproduced)

Komar and Melamid (Vitaly Komar; Russian; b. 1943, Moscow, Russia; lives and works in New York, NY; Alex Melamid, Russian; b. 1945, Moscow, Russia; lives and works in New York, NY)
*The People's Choice*, 1995
Silkscreen on paper (6)
26 1/2 x 19 inches
Courtesy of Alex Melamid
(pl. 45)

Jeff Koons (American; b. 1955, York, PA; lives and works in New York, NY)
*Inflatable Flower and Bunny (Tall White, Pink Bunny)*, 1979
Vinyl, mirrors
32 x 25 x 19 inches
The Broad Art Foundation
(pl. 11)

Jeff Koons (American; b. 1955, York, PA; lives and works in New York, NY)
*Balloon Dog (Blue)*, 2002
Porcelain, edition of 2300 plus 50 APs
10 1/2 x 10 1/2 x 5 inches
Courtesy of Dr. and Mrs. Barry Silverman
(pl. 12)

Joseph Kosuth (American, b. 1945, Toledo, OH; lives and works in London, England)
*An Object Self-Defined*, 1966
Orange neon mounted on wall
4 x 68 inches
Courtesy of the artist and Sprüth Magers
(pl. 8)

Rachel Lachowicz (American; b. 1964, San Francisco, CA; lives and works in Claremont, CA)
*Untitled (Lipstick Urinals)*, 1992
Lipstick, wax, plaster, fiberglass
15 x 9 x 6 inches
From the Private Collection of Richard and Elyse Froehlich
Courtesy Shoshana Wayne Gallery
(pl. 7)

Elad Lassry (Israeli; b. 1977, Tel Aviv, Israel; lives and works in Los Angeles, CA)
*Man*, 2007
C-print, edition 5 of 5 plus 2 APs
14 x 11 inches
Rubell Family Collection, Miami
(pl. 17)

Elad Lassry (Israeli; b. 1977,
Tel Aviv, Israel; lives and works
in Los Angeles, CA)
*Czech Girl*, 2009
C-print, edition 3 of 5 plus 2 APs
14 x 11 inches
Rubell Family Collection, Miami
(pl. 18)

Elad Lassry (Israeli; b. 1977,
Tel Aviv, Israel; lives and works
in Los Angeles, CA)
*Lipstick*, 2009
C-print
14 x 11 inches
Rubell Family Collection, Miami
(pl. 19)

Elad Lassry (Israeli; b. 1977,
Tel Aviv, Israel; lives and works
in Los Angeles, CA)
*Selkirk Rex, LaPerm*, 2011
C-print, diptych, edition 4 of 5
14 ½ x 11 ½ inches (each)
Rubell Family Collection, Miami
(pl. 20)

Sherrie Levine (American; b. 1947,
Hazelton, PA; lives and works
in New York, NY and Santa Fe, NM)
*Fountain (Buddha)*, 1996
Bronze
12 x 17 x 16 inches
The Institute of Contemporary Art/
Boston. Gift of Barbara Lee,
The Barbara Lee Collection of Art
by Women
(pl. 5)

Jorge Pardo (Cuban-American; b. 1963,
Havana, Cuba; lives and works
in Los Angeles, CA)
*Palette*, 1990
Oak wood, 16 penny nails, Danish oil
40 x 27 ¼ x 5 inches
Collection Thomas Solomon and
Kimberly Mascola
(pl. 13)

Jorge Pardo (Cuban-American; b. 1963,
Havana, Cuba; lives and works
in Los Angeles, CA)
*Le Corbusier Chair*, 1990
Welded copper pipes
26 x 30 x 33 ¼ inches
Courtesy of de la Cruz Collection,
Miami, FL
(pl. 14)

Jorge Pardo (Cuban-American; b. 1963,
Havana, Cuba; lives and works
in Los Angeles, CA)
*Le Corbusier Sofa*, 1990
Welded copper pipes
26 x 64 x 30 inches
Courtesy of de la Cruz Collection,
Miami, FL
(pl. 15)

Richard Pettibone (American; b. 1938,
Alhambra, CA; lives and works
in Los Angeles, CA)
*The Blind Man*, 2015
Oil on canvas (6)
5 ⅞ x 5 inches
7 ½ x 6 1/4 inches
8 ¾ x 7 ½ inches
10 ¼ x 8 ¾ inches
11 ⅝ x 10 inches
14 ¼ x 11 ¾ inches
Courtesy Castelli Gallery, New York
(pl. 4)

Richard Phillips (American; b. 1962,
Marblehead, MA; lives and works
in New York, NY)
*Jacko (after Jeff Koons)*, 1998
Oil on linen
99 x 78 x 3 inches
The Collection of Dillon L. Cohen
(pl. 49)

Richard Phillips (American; b. 1962,
Marblehead, MA; lives and works
in New York, NY)
*Fiktive Models I*, 2016
Oil on linen
108 x 73 ⅛ inches
Courtesy Gagosian
(pl. 50)

Richard Phillips (American; b. 1962,
Marblehead, MA; lives and works
in New York, NY)
*Fiktive Models IV*, 2016
Oil on linen
108 x 72 inches
The Collection of John & Amy Phelan
(pl. 51)

Francis Picabia (French; 1879–1953)
*L'Andalusia*, ca. 1941–42
Oil on canvas
41 ¾ x 29 ⅞ inches
Jeff and Mei Sze Greene Collection
(pl. 25)

Francis Picabia (French; 1879–1953)
*Don Quichotte*, ca. 1941–42
Oil and ink on cardboard
37 ¾ x 29 ⅞ inches
Jeff and Mei Sze Greene Collection
(pl. 26)

Julian Schnabel (American; b. 1951, Brooklyn, NY; lives and works in New York, NY)
*Veramente Bestia V (Girl with No Eyes)*, 1988
Oil on found object
19 ¾ x 15 ¾ inches
Courtesy of the artist
(pl. 27)

Tom Scicluna (British; b. 1974, London, England; lives and works in Miami, FL)
*Ordinance No. C-14-23*, 2014
Neon sign and fixtures
20 x 37 x 3 inches
NSU Art Museum Fort Lauderdale; purchased with funds provided by Michael and Diane Bienes by exchange
(pl. 28)

Alfred Stieglitz (1864–1946)
*Fountain*, 1917
Photograph of *Fountain* by Marcel Duchamp (1887–1968)
Printed in *The Blind Man*, no. 2 (May 1917)
11 x 8 1/16 inches
The Metropolitan Museum of Art, New York, Thomas J. Watson Library (Purchased with income from the Jacob S. Rogers Fund)
(pl. 1)

Kara Walker (American; b. 1969, Stockton, CA; lives and works in New York, NY)
*Untitled*, 1994
Paper on canvas
10 x 10 x ¾ inches
NSU Art Museum Fort Lauderdale; Promised Gift of David Horvitz and Francie Bishop Good
(pl. 47)

Kara Walker (American; b. 1969, Stockton, CA; lives and works in New York, NY)
*Untitled*, 1994
Paper on canvas
10 x 10 x ¾ inches
NSU Art Museum Fort Lauderdale; Promised Gift of David Horvitz and Francie Bishop Good
(pl. 48)

Andy Warhol (American; 1928–1987)
*Brillo Soap Pads Box*, 1964
Silkscreen ink and house paint on plywood
17 x 17 x 14 inches
The Andy Warhol Museum, Pittsburgh; Founding Collection, Contribution The Andy Warhol Foundation for the Visual Arts, Inc.
(pl. 9)

Andy Warhol (American; 1928–1987)
*Heinz Tomato Ketchup Box*, 1964
Silkscreen ink and house paint on plywood
8 ½ x 15 ½ x 10 ½ inches
The Andy Warhol Museum, Pittsburgh; Founding Collection, Contribution The Andy Warhol Foundation for the Visual Arts, Inc.
(not reproduced)

Andy Warhol (American; 1928–1987)
*Campbell's Tomato Juice Box*, 1964
Silkscreen ink and house paint on plywood
10 x 19 x 9 ½ inches
The Andy Warhol Museum, Pittsburgh; Founding Collection, Contribution The Andy Warhol Foundation for the Visual Arts, Inc.
(pl. 10)

Andy Warhol (American; 1928–1987)
*Del Monte Peach Halves Box*, 1964
Silkscreen ink and house paint on plywood
12 x 15 x 9 ½ inches
The Andy Warhol Museum, Pittsburgh; Founding Collection, Contribution The Andy Warhol Foundation for the Visual Arts, Inc.
(not reproduced)

Andy Warhol (American; 1928–1987)
*Campbell's Soup II: Scotch Broth*, 1969
Serigraph, edition 249 of 250
35 x 23 inches
NSU Art Museum Fort Lauderdale; Gift of Mr. Irving Luntz
(not reproduced)

# Photography Credits

*Plates*
1: © Succession Marcel Duchamp / ADAGP, Paris / Artists Rights Society (ARS), New York 2017; The Metropolitan Museum of Art, New York, Thomas J. Watson Library
2: © Succession Marcel Duchamp / ADAGP, Paris / Artists Rights Society (ARS), New York 2017; Collection of Pérez Art Museum Miami, Photo by Sid Hoeltzell
3: © Succession Marcel Duchamp / ADAGP, Paris / Artists Rights Society (ARS), New York 2017; Collection of The John and Mable Ringling Museum of Art, the State Art Museum of Florida, Florida State University, Sarasota, Florida
4: © Richard Pettibone; Courtesy of Castelli Gallery, New York, NY
5: Courtesy the artist and David Zwirner New York/London. © Sherrie Levine
6: © Mike Bidlo; Francis M. Naumann Fine Art, LLC
7: © Rachel Lachowicz; Photograph: Gene Ogami; Courtesy Shoshana Wayne Gallery, Los Angeles, CA
8: © 2017 Joseph Kosuth / Artists Rights Society (ARS), New York; Courtesy of the artist and Sprüth Magers
9–10: © 2017 The Andy Warhol Foundation for the Visual Arts, Inc. / Artists Rights Society (ARS), New York; The Andy Warhol Museum, Pittsburgh; Founding Collection, Contribution The Andy Warhol Foundation for the Visual Arts, Inc.
11–12: © Jeff Koons; Courtesy the artist and The Broad Art Foundation
13–15: © Jorge Pardo; Courtesy of the Artist and Petzel Gallery, New York
16: © Cory Arcangel; Courtesy Cory Arcangel and Team (Gallery, Inc.)
17–20: © Elad Lassry; Rubell Family Collection, Miami
21–24: © Steven Baldi. Courtesy the artist and Koenig & Clinton, New York. Photo: Steven Baldi, Los Angeles
25–26: Francis Picabia © 2017 Artists Rights Society (ARS), New York / ADAGP, Paris; Jeff and Mei Sze Greene Collection
27: © 2017 Julian Schnabel / Artists Rights Society (ARS), New York; Courtesy of the artist
28: © Tom Scicluna; Courtesy of the artist

29: © Claire Fontaine, Courtesy of Galerie Chantal Crousel and Air de Paris, Paris; Photo: Sebastiano Pellion
30: © Courtesy John Baldessari, 1972, Edizioni Toselli, Milano; Rosemary Furtak Collection, Walker Art Center Library
31–40: © Judy Fiskin; Courtesy of the artist
41: © Estate of Bernd and Hilla Becher; photo by Adam Reich
42–44: Sophie Calle © 2017 Artists Rights Society (ARS), New York / ADAGP, Paris; Courtesy Paula Cooper Gallery and Galerie Perrotin; Installation view at Centre Pompidou
45: © Vitaly Komar and Alex Melamid; Courtesy of Alex Melamid
46: © 2017 Mike Kelley Foundation for the Arts. All Rights Reserved / Licensed by VAGA, New York, NY; Rubell Family Collection, Miami
47–48: © Kara Walker; Courtesy of Sikkema Jenkins & Co., New York
49–51: © Richard Phillips; Courtesy Gagosian
52: © Samson Kambalu ; Courtesy of the artist and Kate MacGarry, London

*Figures*
1–2: Collection Jean-Jacques Lebel, Paris
3: *The New York Herald*, April 11, 1917
4: Jacques Villon © 2017 Artists Rights Society (ARS), New York / ADAGP, Paris; Photo: Minneapolis Institute of Art
5: Walt Kuhn, Kuhn family papers, and Armory Show records, Archives of American Art, Smithsonian Institution, Washington, DC
6: Walter Pach Papers, 1857–1980, Archives of American Art, Smithsonian Institution, Washington, DC
7: *Vanity Fair* (September 1915): p. 57; Photograph courtesy of Francis M. Naumann